SOUTH AFRICA
REFLECTIONS ON A REVOLUTION

From Zulu Beginnings To Current Events

Donough McGillycuddy

Copyright © Donough McGillycuddy 2017
This book is sold subject to the condition that it shall not, by way of trade or otherwise, be lent, resold, hired out, or otherwise circulated without the publisher's prior consent in any form of binding or cover other than that in which it is published and without a similar condition including this condition being imposed on the subsequent publisher.
The moral right of Donough McGillycuddy has been asserted.
ISBN-13: 978-1976381089
ISBN-10: 1976381088

*In memory of Wendy, mother of our children:
Piers, Lavinia, Michael, and Jocelyn.*

Information in this book is true and complete to the best of author's knowledge. This book is presented solely for educational and informative purposes. The author disclaims any liability in connection with the use of this information or with respect to any loss or incidental or consequential damages caused, or alleged to have been caused, directly or indirectly, by the information contained herein.

CONTENTS

INTRODUCTION 1
CHAPTER I. *Marikana* 10
CHAPTER II. *History* 32
CHAPTER III. *Shaka* 37
CHAPTER IV. *Civil War* 41
CHAPTER V. *The People* 47
CHAPTER VI. *Breakout From Cape Colony* 58
CHAPTER VII. *The Battles* 61
CHAPTER VIII. *Major Political And Industrial Changes* 68
CHAPTER IX. *Civil Strife* 71
CHAPTER X. *Industrial Relations* 86
CHAPTER XI. *Eskom* 99
CHAPTER XII. *Agriculture* 114
CHAPTER XIII. *Hunting* 129
CHAPTER XIV. *Financial Matters* 135
CHAPTER XV. *Education* 159
CHAPTER XVI. *Summary* 165
EPILOGUE 173
SEQUEL 183

ACKNOWLEDGMENTS

Wendy, my late wife, for script reading and suggesting corrections; my late father for sending me to Eton; M'tutor there, A.J. Marsden and my classical tutor, D.H. McIndoe; George Bizos S.C., for permission to eulogise his amazing life and legal career; Pat Eustace, my neighbouring farmer in KwaZulu-Natal for the loan of Dr Bryant's THE ZULU PEOPLE and THE DIARY OF HENRY FYNN; Heather Hannaway, of Schuter and Shooter (publishers of those works); my former brother officer, Major General Sir Robert Corbett, KCVO, CB, Commandant in Berlin when the wall came down; Stephen King for ON WRITING; The Editor of *The Witness*, *SA Farmer's Weekly* and the *Daily Telegraph* for publishing so many of my letters; Gordon and Anne Knox at Underberg Computer Centre; Jimmy Wales (*Nupedia*) and Larry Sanger for creating *Wikipedia*, Larry Page and Sergey Brin for creating *Google*; eminent Irish author, Marjorie Quarton for her course on Creative Writing, and all those who said "***you ought to write a book!***" I say, "Thank you, Tapadh leat, Merci beaucoup and Ngibonga kakhulu."

INTRODUCTION

South Africa's Public Protector, Mrs Thuli Madonsela, found that Jacob Zuma, the President, had unduly benefitted from upgrades at the taxpayer's expense to his personal homestead of Nkandla and that he should repay the Exchequer for the non-security upgrades. Early in 2017, a Parliamentary Committee formed exclusively from the President's African National Congress Party, absolved the President of any wrong-doing.

Mr Zuma appears in the vanguard of South African corruption. Where the leader leads, many of the people follow. 83% of South Africans believe that corruption has become worse in the last year, according to Transparency International.

"What to some is food, to others may be sharp poison," wrote Lucretius in *De rerum Natura*, a work written at the time of the Roman invasion of Britain that had considerable influence on the writings by Virgil of *The Aeneid* and *Georgics*. Read on and your knowledge of South Africa and what is happening there today will be second only to what Roman philosophers knew about their world.

A lot of information in this book is garnered from A. T. Bryant, D. Litt., author of THE ZULU PEOPLE, his greatest work which he completed in 1935 before retiring back to England from being a Missionary in Zululand. The Preface of his two volumes opens with the words: *"The importance of this work may not be fully realised at the present moment."*

Well, I realise its importance and bring to light afresh the lives of a people who have undergone a past phenomenal revolution and who live in a country where a revolution is in the making. When the Reverend Dr Bryant lived amongst the Zulus, about 1883 to 1933, the pastoral Zulu had seen little change to his lifestyle in a few hundred years. When the Portuguese came inland in 1589 they found the people somewhere between the European Stone and Iron ages. They lived in beautifully constructed beehive huts of mud walls and thatched roofs. They are still building to a similar design, the size of the door and galvanised tin roofs being the fundamental differences. The Zulu has stuck with his design despite seeing the European settler continuously advancing architecture and engineering.

South Africa is in its infancy as a developing nation. Dr Bryant clearly gives the impression that the Zulu race has come a long way in the last 200 years. They and the other indigenous races were evolving from the Bantu-Nguni tribes about the time of the Battle of Waterloo, 1815. The history of their evolution was kept verbally in the absence of any physical means of recording it. They did not have ink, paper, canvas or paint brushes. There is a great gap between the rock-art drawings in the caves of the San people and anything recorded two thousand years later. One animal, the largest member of the antelope (*Tragelaphus*) species, spans that gap. The Eland appears in many rock 'paintings' and we see them in the bergs with a pleasant degree of frequency today. The animal is virtually unchanged; the people are changing fast, very fast. In a century plus, their barefoot dress has changed from hunted-animal leather girdles to textile European-style shirts, trousers and shoes. Their traditional life has largely passed into obscurity yet the larder of rural people has not enlarged very much. The arrival of Kentucky Fried Chicken in a rural town has met with mixed response. The Zulu prefers snacks and beer in a shabeen.

Mid-C.19th King Shaka organised the Bantu-Nguni tribes, scattered from the Harrismith and Ladysmith area to Durban, into one powerful nation, upgrading their weaponry and fighting methods. By the time Cetshwayo led them they were the finest standing army that ever contested imperial British rule. Their defeat by the British at Ulundi triggered the turn of the tide and the break-up of the Zulu nation and it is now a country of many races that have made Kwazulu-Natal their home. The name of the province may be translated, 'Natal, the home of the Zulu.'

The book contains a number of digressions into contemporary European life which is designed to aid the reader to more fully understand 'the nature of the beast.' The placid native can turn very nasty in a very short time if provoked. There is an old genealogical saying that *"if you don't know where you have been, how can you know where you are going?"* Well, the book tells us where the Zulu has been but does not reveal where the people of South Africa are going. The author is not in the 'Prediction Business', as an attorney once advised him. The recent affair (2013) of the Sahara computer-owning Guptas landing a civilian Airbus 330-200 without proper authorisation at a key point military airbase for a family wedding at Sun City says much about the respect for law and order within the South African government's corridors of power. It was one of those rare incidents for which three Generals, one Colonel and ten police officers were immediately suspended. *"If you must break the law, do it to seize power, in all other cases observe it,"* said Julius Caesar. Law-breaking, corruption, crime, rape and murder are deeply ingrained in the native psyche and it makes little difference to race or colour. Accountability for wrong-doing is widely avoided. Responsibility is accepted, zealously guarded and as quickly discarded with frequent consultation with the ancestors. Individual success can be resented and the person reprimanded for not taking the family-group into closer consideration. The old codes of higher moral conduct have disappeared as fast as drugs have affected the minds of those who get hooked. The ravage of HIV-Aids has left a lot of one-parent and child-dependent families. The extension of anti-retroviral treatment has been a great success with life expectancy increasing 50% in many cases.

An overall view of the people at large gives an impression of their general contentment. Too few are employed and there is no great expectancy of the improvement of their lot through hard work by very many. The Zulu is creative in small ways yet not recognised for having created anything of significance. Many are hardworking and delightful to work with. However, joinery, the use of animal dung as fertiliser and the pack ox for carrying have not been used by them as effectively as this imparted knowledge has been with other races. They use their initiative most commendably yet a benefactor's life can be ended as quickly and tragically, as was the case with the late David Rattray. Their temperament can be volatile and it is difficult to tell what will follow the toyi-toyi, ululating, singing and dancing. It is usually tear gas grenades and rubber bullets. The Arab Spring has descended geographically as far south as the Central African Republic and Malawi. Only Zimbabwe stands between the latter and South Africa.

The second definition of the word Revolution in the Oxford

English Dictionary, after 'revolving', gives 'complete change, turning upside-down, great reversal of conditions, fundamental reconstruction' *et cetera*. The needs of people and their views on matters are amongst the characteristics that define races all over the world. In the early 2000s, homosexuality in Uganda was curbed by the death penalty whereas in the Western world, governments seek to accommodate same-sex items in the same manner as the centuries-old custom of institutional monogamous marriage. France is the latest example. It barely matters where the country is, revolution is taking place in some form and in varying degrees. Worldwide, unemployment, hunger, absence of leadership, or excessive zeal therein unsettles people and they take the law into their own hands. Simply put, they have a revolution on their hands.

The most recent warning to South Africans that '*securocrats, the plundering of the public purse* (now termed State Capture) *and the attack on our democratic institutions*' could '*create imbalance where law and justice cannot be reconciled with morality as our institutions and the very laws themselves will be perceived to be illegitimate,*' comes from Greek-born 84-year-old Senior Counsel, George Bizos. Who is he?

George Bizos was born in Vasilitsi on the Messinian peninsula of the Peleponese. His father, Antoni, was Mayor of the small village in Nazi-occupied Greece during the early part of WW2. His primary school was a helot of the original Spartans who were renowned for their austerity and hardiness. The culture lasted the boy a lifetime during which these traits were at times very necessary. At the age of 13 George would not abandon his father when helping seven New Zealand soldiers, whose names are on Wikipedia, to escape from Greece to Crete. All did not go according to plan. After three days adrift in the Mediterranean, along comes a British J and K class Destroyer whose name augured well for the boy's future. It was on H.M.S. *Kimberley* that the teenager first saw action against the enemy, being fascinated with the conveyor belt system that brought shells to the ack-ack guns fending off German Ju 87 Stuka dive-bombers. Not wishing the little Greek boy any harm, the sailors sent him down to the safety of the Ward room. Kimberley's sister ship was H.M.S. Kelly, commanded by Lord Louis Mountbatten.

After the Battle for Crete, the destroyer dropped him off at Alexandria. As a refugee he was sent to South Africa, landed in

Durban and thence went by train to Johannesburg. Arriving just as the Ossewabrandwag were demonstrating their anger about European *vuilgoed* (rubbish) being brought to South Africa by Jan Smuts, he was absorbed into the local Greek community. Speaking neither English nor Afrikaans, young George could not immediately go to school but by 1948, the year the National Party was voted into power, maturing George had managed to gain entry into the law faculty at the University of Witwatersrand. He joined the Johannesburg Bar in 1954. Denied a passport until 1972, he was not able to return to his native Greece for many years of apartheid. During the 1950s and 60s he was Advocate to a wide range of well-known people including Bishop Trevor Huddleston, KCMG, of Sophiatown, Johannesburg. Engraved on the stone supporting the Bishop's bust in his birthplace of Bedford, England, are the words of Nelson Mandela's eulogy to him, "*No white person has done more for South Africa than Trevor Huddleston.*"

At the Rivonia Trial in 1963-4, Advocate George Bizos was part of the team that defended Nelson Mandela, Govan Mbeki and Walter Sisulu. Bizos is almost universally admired, particularly by indigenous people for his selflessness and the hours he sacrificed defending natives facing serious political charges that could even have resulted in some of his clients being sentenced to death. *Madiba could not have been a client of the now-famous Senior Counsel at Legal Resources Centre if he had been sentenced to death*, wrote Phillip Mtimkulu of Pretoria in the Durban *Mercury* on 24th April, 2013. Mandela said in his famous speech at his trial that he was prepared to die "*if needs be*", words suggested by Bizos which had the effect of the accused not appearing to seek martyrdom and consequently being sentenced to life imprisonment instead of the death penalty. He was later leader of the team for the SA government to argue that the death penalty was unconstitutional.

George Bizos went on to lead the team that opposed applications for amnesty on behalf of Biko, Hani, Goniwe, Calata, Mkhonto, Mhlauli, Slovo and Schoon families. He received the Order for Meritorious Service, Class II medal from President Mandela, the International Trial Lawyer Prize of the year, 2001, from the International Academy of Trial Lawyers and the Bernard Simmons Memorial Award, 2004, from the International Bar Association.

He led the team from Legal Resources Centre in the Farlam Inquiry and it appears that a full day's work was barely enough for him at the age of eighty-four. Hence when someone of his stature and experience states that South Africa must choose between the road leading to the plundering of State resources, or the more difficult road which would lead the country to a place where its laws were respected and where those who broke them were acted against, it is time for the people to listen. He recognised that youth was replacing the 'old guard' and that it would be worthwhile discussing how the national institutions can be strengthened. Working together in the common purpose of binding ourselves to the nation's just laws and to act against those who break them are in the country's national best interests. It could be folly for political leaders to discard the wisdom expressed at the School of Practical Philosophy. "*Despite some criticism,*" said the octogenarian 'guru' of South African law, "*in the main, we are governed by democratically elected representatives and have an independent judiciary, but this does not mean that these institutions should not be constantly regulated by the citizenry.*" The success or failure of the South African Revolution now in progress is dependent upon adhering to such advice. Of his three sons, two are eminent surgeons in England and the third has a mechanical engineering business in JNB. What a story; what a man, a lot stronger than Johnnie Walker!

There are many more recipe books than ones with a foreboding assessment of current affairs and the highly probable outcome. This book is written without motivation by someone who went full of bright expectation to live in South Africa eight years after democracy came about. It is necessary to tell again in a different light the story, sometimes in gruesome and graphic detail, so that the reader gathers fundamental knowledge of the people involved in today's revolution. Focus is upon the Zulu, the most formidable of native tribes. The white man gets less mention because he is the least likely person to be involved and accepts revolution simply as the changing pattern of things over which he has little or no control. There are plenty of other tribes. It must be remembered that the President is a Zulu and a direct descendant of the people mostly written about. South Africa is a magnificent large country peopled by original natives of the highest physical quality anywhere. They are not Caucasian, they are not Australasian, or American, or Asian. They are descendants of the Bantu – Nguni people who were found by European explorers to be of the Northern Hemisphere Stone Age or Iron Age. Anyone thinking that these people should have the intellect which the Caucasian Europeans have acquired over thousands of years of cultural and academic education is hemispherically deluded. It is irrational to think that the South African black native thinks the same as a white European and to comment without qualification on the difference. It places the speaker in a category of those who have not taken full advantage of the education that they have been given, sometimes at great expense. The author could scarcely wish for better people to live and work with than our domestic maid, Saraphina Radebe, and our gardener-handyman, Mduduzi Mzolo, that formed his homestead team. They are as good timekeepers as a John Bunting C.18th clock and as reliable as the day is long.

Since the ANC ousted Thabo Mbeki at Polokwane (*Place of Safety*, formerly Pietersburg) in December 2007 in favour of Jacob Zuma, the writer's views changed. The recipes for roasting chicken or baking bread are similar all over the world. The recipes for revolution or civil war are similar all over the world. Poverty, hunger, unemployment and mediocre leadership by those elected are as common to prospective strife as flour, yeast, salt, sugar and water are to a plain loaf. In the chapters that follow it can be clearly seen that the ingredients are in the dough and the baker's hand is on the oven door. If it seems that too heavy emphasis is placed upon Eskom, the national electrical power supplier, it is not without reason. When one thinks about it there is nothing much that has been done in the last century without electricity. There are few things that mankind is now so dependent on. We charge our cell phones, heat the water, run a tap, use computers, laptops, electric lights, heating and swimming pool pumps to name a few domestic uses. Nine percent of electricity generated in South Africa is used in heavy industries like smelting, mining and engineering. No other industry is capable of either holding the government to ransom or failing in its duty to supply the people with power. No other industry is being watched so closely by potential investors in South Africa. Murders, crime, car accidents, corruption and rhino poaching take second place when there is anything about Eskom to be reported in the media. As the winter of 2013-4 set in, Eskom's finances were in such a parlous state that the new billing contains four extra headings putting nearly R40 per day on the average domestic consumer's bill. Should one be even a few hundred rand overdue, disconnection was threatened. That smacks in the face of the assurance from the National Electricity Regulator that Eskom will conduct its business in the best interests of consumers who are heavily subsidising manufacturing industries such as BHP Billiton.

The hierarchy of human needs is largely based upon the needs of both moral and physical life. The prime desire for recognition does not put bread on the table or a roof over a tenement. Where colonial powers sought to gain from their exploration in new lands, they required subjugated native labour to gather the crops, package them and execute delivery to a port, often by slow ox-wagon. For a long time the unpaid labourer was known as a slave yet he/she was not completely unpaid. The producer who intended maximising profit from an exploration realised that even slaves could be coerced with a carrot as an alternative to being beaten like an ox with a stick. The notion that reward brought favourable results brought about the existence of collective dwellings near the workplace.

As the wider international world developed, a labourer and his/her output became both a human resource and a saleable commodity, a feature that transcended into the slave trade. Countries of the new world were sparsely populated and the American-Indian certainly was not going to be caught and shackled by the early colonialists from the East. Each had totally different social systems and 'Reserves' exist to this day as points where ancient culture is preserved. The two features shared by East and West remained principally food and shelter. Where food was provided it formed subsistence, fuel for the body that would be used to smash stones for the formation of roads and much later railroads. I saw recently a puzzle that fell from a Christmas cracker. "Why did man always go west?" My guess is that he followed the sun, particularly in the Northern Hemisphere of greater land mass. The Englishman's notion has been to explore south and west, after all, the further north he went the colder it got. The adventure gene developed much earlier in some civilisations than others and we are left with legacies that we do not altogether understand such as the Great Pyramids, Stonehenge and the Mayan temples in both Eastern and Western worlds of the Southern Hemisphere, neither of which peoples knew the other.

Over the ensuing few thousand years matters became more orderly, there were industrial revolutions and increasing formalisation of the productive work ethic. Some of the rich became very rich, many in the upper echelons of society displayed their enrichment through property and very many more experienced only the marginal gain from their labour, never being quite sure if they lived to work or worked to live. The story of THE SCRAMBLE FOR AFRICA is well recounted by Thomas Pakenham. The scramble is far from over. It just takes a different form whilst the ebb and flow of trade to a great extent dictates the relative value of national currency. When the currency is weak speculators scramble for value for money and exports become cheaper where sold. Matters stabilise in a strong currency as the risks attached to investment diminish. The author's quest is to record the nature of the people and the problems they face. They live in a most beautiful country whose plains, seascapes and mountain views give enormous aesthetic pleasure. Wildlife abounds in many national and private game parks. The natives are friendly, the food excellent, all tourist accommodation very clean and comfortable with welcoming hosts. The currency can be volatile and visits are best made when ZAR10 = US$1, ZAR15 = GBP1 and ZAR13 = €1. The same goes for property and the www.pamgolding.co.za website is well worth a glance to see what is available for as little as R2m. [S200,000; £133,000; or €153,846]. In February 2015, the rand, @ R11.88 : US$1 is at its weakest since 2002.

The book contains a modicum of international history, especially European, so that the non-African reader may better understand South Africa's revolution. It will also help the South African to better understand what has happened in other countries and the subtle differences between the natives of different lands.

©McGillycuddy, Himeville, 08/07/2013, with one amendment (Currency exchange rate) on 12/02/2015. Some further amendments made at Nenagh in February 2017.

CHAPTER I

MARIKANA

Until 16th August 2012 only a very small proportion of the world's population had ever heard of the name. It is now etched on the world map in the same letters as Sharpville (69), Bolpatong (45) and Lellefontein (35). The numbers in parenthesis are of those massacred and with the total of 44 killed in the Marikana area during that fateful week, big questions are being asked and a retired Supreme Court judge by the name of Ian Farlam had until 31st May to wrap up the judicial Commission of Inquiry. Rather than pre-empt who will be 'fingered', it may be best to study the circumstances surrounding the event. President Jacob Zuma called the Commission of Inquiry and it is he who has taken the unprecedented step of pre-empting the findings of Judge Farlam's Commission. The President announced at Davos at the end of January that Lonmin were to blame for the affair for negotiating with some workers outside the formal bargaining system, thus causing excluded workers to resort to wildcat strikes.

I have read frequently about the magnificence of the South African wage bargaining system. Smooth operation is ensured from the end of one wage settlement until the following year's one is tabled. It is only South Africa that prides itself on the excellence of employer-labour relations. The World Economic Forum meeting this time in Cape Town describes them as the worst in the world. Having been so successful in mining and in agriculture, workers now perceive wildcat strikes as an effective and legitimate means of seeking wage increases. The recent track record of success may *"increase their prevalence and intensity"* said Charles Laurie, an African analyst at UK-based *Maplecroft*. The NUM warned that it would demand of the Chamber of Mines double-digit wage increases against the backdrop of

5.9% 'inflation'. In a timely reminder, Pravin Gordhan (Finance Minister) reminded workers who might have been at home listening to the morning radio that workers should appreciate that a wage increase above inflation creates an expectancy of higher production. He implied that too high a proportion of workers expected more pay for the same output and that insufficient numbers were prepared to take pride in menial jobs such as brick-laying. When it is universally recognised that poor education is the root cause of potential employees being unfit for a job, the teachers handed in a litany of demands to the President's office warning of a full-blown strike and disruption of mid-year examinations if their demands are not met within weeks. Where 30% achievement in examination results is now the norm, does it make any difference whether pupils sit exams or not?

A modicum of the South African working population came into focus last August (2014) when rock-drill operators were perceived as receiving inadequate remuneration for the dirty job that they do and the squalor in which they live far from their real homes. Doing something drastic can be good. It is necessary to ensure that the consequences are acceptable to a wider audience. When some are seen to profit from an independent action, others will liken their situation to that of the beneficiary and jump on the bandwagon. Some were sufficiently naïve to think that, if the miners got more, they were a special case, merited the increase and anyway, "mining is different".

As to the part played by the *izinyanga* as before Marikana with their *intelezi* which was supposed to protect the miners from the effect of bullets fired by the police. I vividly recollect a quick conversation in passing with a friend outside The Highlander Centre in Underberg. In response to my cue that yesterday had been a bad day for South Africa, my friend responded to the effect that the miners were on muthi. The following day (18th Aug) *The Witness* carried an article headed MARIKANA MUTHI and why the Strikers felt invincible. The following day *Sunday Times* ran the story that muti 'protected' miners, citing a mystery Sangoma as being believed to be behind the foolish courage displayed by striking miners before many were massacred. Union officials, residents of Marikana and police confirmed the presence of an unidentified Sangoma (witch doctor) who carried out rituals on the hill and dished out muti where workers had gathered throughout the week. The surviving miners said nothing. It was said that a man from Eastern Cape had provided muti to the protesters and made them believe that it would make them invisible. It cost R500 to have an open cut made with a razor blade sprinkled with *ntelezi*. The miners selected for interview declined to comment. A senior policeman said that they had recorded the muti rituals on camera from a helicopter. *"One by one, in a queue, they were sprinkled with muti."* A young man who refused to be identified believed that but for the muti ritual that prevented bullets hitting people, the death toll would have been a lot higher. Another told *Sunday Times, "they can't be shot, because a strong ritual makes it impossible for them to be hit by a bullet."* – *"If a person got shot despite being 'worked on' he must have done something wrong to weaken the muti."*

Dumisani Nkalitshana, national organiser of the AMCU (Association of Mineworkers and Construction Union), said that they had not heard of any of their members speaking of the muti ritual and that as Christians they believe in God. Police Minister, Nathi Mthethwa, said that the Sangoma who supplied muti to miners making them believe that they would be invisible and immortal, should be called to account. The pursuit by the police to 'finish off' wounded protesters has its precedents and is known to some as 'forward panic'. A massacre resulting from a forward panic is a killing frenzy by perpetrators carried away psychologically in an orgy of violence. At Nanking in 1937, Japanese soldiers killed disarmed Chinese soldiers and civilians. U.S. infantrymen murdered many Vietnamese villagers at My Lai in 1968. During WW2 the Russians murdered thousands of Poles, the Germans millions of Jews and the Japanese hundreds of British prisoners of war working on railways as portrayed in *Bridge over the River Kwai*.

The Commission of Inquiry comprising retired Supreme Court Judge Ian Farlam, Bantubonke Tokata, S.C. and Pingla Hemraj S.C. is charged with investigating all aspects of the massacre following disgruntled workers turning into bloodthirsty thugs. There is no escaping the fact that the lot of the South African miner in the Rustenburg area is not a happy one. The Commission may find that consultations with rock-drill operators, the men at the sharp end, were inadequate.

It is hard to know what conclusions may be drawn from such a small diversity of stories and an apparent abysmal performance by the police. *The truth will come to light* wrote William Shakespeare in Act ii, *The Merchant of Venice*, and so Judge Farlam revisited the area near shaft K3 of the Marikana mine, Rustenburg, to get a clear view of where two policemen were hacked to death days before the massacre and three miners were also killed.

Consoling the sister of Warrant Officer Tsietsi Hendrik Monene, the Judge said, *"Your brother would have been very proud of you."* I think it is the sister who should be very proud of her brother who was sent into an extremely difficult situation accompanied by another officer and no cover that anyone has spoken of. Many have said of the miners, *"You don't go butchering policemen and hope to get away with it!"* Agreed, but for the fact that the situation may already have been out of control for reasons going back a considerable distance in time. Living conditions, wages, pay-day debt, sociological circumstances had all manifested themselves into general dissatisfaction with life in the minds of the miners and they were agitated and restless. The truth will come to light.

That which hits agriculture in the form of such a large rise in the basic minimum wage can be expected to hit other industries. Almost total confusion prevailed as wildcat strikes continued to cause five Exxaro-managed power station collieries to be idle for the past two weeks. The workers on strike were members of the National Union of Mineworkers and they have ignored a union call to return to work. Members of other unions were not on strike. The workers went on strike over non-payment of bonuses or performance incentives – unpaid as production targets had not been achieved. The union suggested that Exxaro might make an across-the-board payment. The company still did not see why it should pay anything for non-performance. They came back with a compromise single payment of 2% of annual salary [equivalent to R 2,000 for each striker] on condition that the workers returned to work immediately. The proposal was rejected by the NUM without it being clear if they had a mandate from the strikers.

The wage gap in 2011 between CEO and average worker in the mining industry was 390:1 *"Blame the wage earner for the country's ills while the top gorges itself,"* says Computus, a forensic accounting firm <http://www.fin24.com/Business/Executive-pay-on-the-top-20100430>. It seems unreasonable to expect the South African worker to tolerate poor pay for much longer. 75% of the working population is employed. That figure may need to fall to 70% or lower before a bottom is found and South Africa again produces goods and services on the world market at a price that is profitable after fair remuneration.

In this the third millennium, the South African Police Service must answer why their actions were totally out of proportion. Police are authorised to use force, but this must be "the minimum force that is reasonable in the circumstances." The police units brought to the front at Marikana were not guided by the principles of common law where an act of self-defence "may not be more harmful than necessary to ward off the attack." They had been trained in a doctrine of maximum force and the cameras captured for the first time the type of concentrated fire that these special units are trained in.

Just one typically South African twist in the tale. Two weeks later it was reported in *The Witness* (Apr. 9th) that Uncedo Service Taxi Association president Ntsikelelo Gaehler said at the Sangoma's funeral in Bizana, near Port Edward, Eastern Cape, that Jolo was killed by members of the taxi industry. He was shot outside his home in Ludeke Halt on 24th March. Gaehler reportedly said, *"It is wrong that we are confusing the family, the community and the police by making them believe the Ndzabe murder was associated with Marikana while we know it was some of us in the industry. We have to talk the truth."*

When they have time to study the matter, some policemen recognise that their 'elite' unit reacted to the crowd of miners at Marikana in an 'exceptional' manner. The country probably thought that the days of mass execution in South Africa had ended with the end of the struggle in 1994. There are a number of things that it is important to remember about the development of the Nguni people and of the country that they live in. Putting time scales into perspective, the horse was first brought into Zululand about 1808 by the returning fugitive chieftain Dingiswayo who got it from some travelling Europeans near the Transvaal Utrecht district. The Peninsular War commenced in Spain that year. It was four years before Napoleon marched on Moscow and seven years before Waterloo. The last elephant was shot on the Berea, the hill above Durban, somewhere between 1846 and 1853, the era of the Great Exhibition in London. The harmless, necessary domestic cat, well-known to the Egyptians deep into B.C., was only introduced to Britain, 800-1,000 A.D. and did not become *iKati* to the Zulus until mid-C.18th. Anyone expecting the descendants of the natural native Nguni tribes to march *paripassu* with Caucasoids has not understood a word of anthropology. It has absolutely nothing to do with race. It is as sure a fact as saying that cats like milk and hate water.

Successive Presidential appointments of the wrong man for the job, Jackie Selebi and Bheki Cele preceded that of a totally inexperienced woman, Riah Phiyega, who rose to the rank of 'General' without a moment's service in any arm. Changes in ideas as to what the police should be, military or civilian, has radically diminished the operational efficiency of the South African Police Service. The people at the top were the political appointees of the man at the top. His knowledge of policing is 100% hearsay. It has nothing to do with experience or suitability for the appointment. In common with most political administrations it's a matter of jobs for one's relations and friends. British Premier Jim Callaghan appointed his son-in-law UK Ambassador to Washington. Nothing wrong with that. Peter Jay was a 1st class sailor and a 2nd class ambassador.

The President might wish the buck to pass his desk and stop at that of long-past President, Doctor H.F. Verwoerd, as brilliantly depicted by Zapiro, *S. Times*, 30/9/2012. It is not going to. Zuma's salvation is Zulu culture wherein blame cannot rest with the individual. Events happen. It is nobody's fault. One who practices polygamy in the third millennium in his late 60s and early 70s can hide behind this façade of "things that happen, take place. It's nobody's fault".

A revolution of thinking is necessary for a top echelon career police officer to be promoted to National Police Commissioner. The same depth of revolution will be necessary to alter the political psyche of the governing party from making political appointments in the field of national security. If people should cause trouble they can be recalled and replaced on a whim. It was careless of the President to appoint one friend who was corrupt and to have to recall (sack) him, only to appoint in his place a second incompetent who was found 'unfit for office' by a Board of Inquiry. The present incumbent, Riah Phiyega, is a reasonably well educated, loyal ANC member whose most significant job to date was sitting on the Presidential Committee for the FIFA World Cup bid. Probably anywhere else in the world, a National Police Commissioner has served a day or more in a service-orientated capacity. Her lack of experience is matched by the grilling that she receives at the Farlam Inquiry into Marikana. I guess that the feminine of fall-guy is 'fall-gal' and I hope for her sake she does not injure herself physically when she hits the deck.

Marikana is symptomatic of the darker side of the beautiful country called South Africa. On the lighter side are the magnificent bergs that can capture a covering of snow in any month of the year, the seascapes of the Eastern, Southern and Western Cape with plunging Southern Right whales and sardine shoal-chasing gannets, the beauty of the 'Garden Route' and the symbolism of the battlefields. Oh there's progress all right, for President Obama came to see it. "*I am making this visit to Africa because I see this as great a moment of progress and great promise for the continent*," said the U.S. President after meeting Senegal's 51-year-old President, Macky Sall in Dakar who replied, "*Africa is a continent that's going somewhere with a strong workforce…we want to offer great opportunities to our young people and grow in prosperity and industry.*" Stirring words which only need translation into jobs for the young people both in Senegal and South Africa. 200 years ago neither people had very much, absolutely nothing of what they have today except their tribal culture and their association with the ancestors. The main point of difference between the two Presidents was that the one from across the pond praised his Supreme Court for ruling that human rights allowed for gay marriages. Gay relationships are against the law in Senegal.

There is a light and a dark side to the moon. By researching in some depth those who have gone before us and become our ancestors, we are in a better position to understand the *Psyché* of the native of South Africa and gain an insight into the reasons for his/her beliefs and actions. If one's ancestors were war-faring, one is likely to be of war-faring disposition. Whilst there are many similarities with the natives of other countries, it is worth noting the differences. When any two people try to resolve their differences, it is helpful to start with what they have in common.

There are not many races around the world that just 180 years ago were ruled by a man who one morning was presented with a baby by one of his seraglios as a compliment of his fecundity. Not being married himself, he did not appreciate the good nature of the presentation and threw the baby in the air with fatal consequences arising from its landing on the hard ground. Many involved at Marikana, both as claimants of rights for a better living wage, and those appointed agents of law and order (SAPS) were descendants of the wonderful Zulu nation forged by the politically astute and militarily savvy King Shaka and of the tribes that evaded being annihilated by his enormous army as he carried out one of the earlier models of ethnic cleansing. Swathes of Zululand from roughly Pietersburg (in the North) to Umtata (in the South) were at one time or another laid waste and devoid of inhabitants. The tribes gathered together by Shaka came from a culture of pastoral people who, when not producing food or hunting, were at war with one another. The English claim that the Irish were always fighting amongst themselves. Just look at the history of the South African tribes!

On one side below the koppie of Marikana, special armed units of well-fed uniformed forces of law and order were assembled, some feeling more than a trifle revengeful at two of their comrades being brutally hacked to death the previous week. On the koppie sat or mingled a very large number of disgruntled workers who do a filthy job in dirty, noisy conditions a long way underground in artificial light and in shifts. Above ground at the end of a shift, washing and cooking facilities are 'basic' in the broad sense of the word. Life in the leaky, draughty shack is cramped and privacy is at a premium and the meal arising suffices to restore most of the day's expended calories. Provision of the carbohydrates necessary to sustain the energy of a rock-face driller should probably be defined as an 'art form'. Possibly 750 calories/hour are used and they have to be replaced every shift-end.

Workers are also a few hundred kilometres from their actual home, a legacy from being dispossessed and located by the Nationalist apartheid government. For their contribution to the South African economy and what they produce for the benefit of shareholders afar off, the money is as poor as the conditions including sanitation and health care. Many do it because it was a way of life for their fathers and ancestors who were hired to dig in large numbers by colonial employers. Diamond finds at Kimberley led to De Beers commandeering the diamond trade. As gold was found near the Jukskei River in the Transvaal, so shacks were erected on top of all that platinum, palladium, silver, gold and other precious metals in what is now Gauteng Province (GP), home to the cities of Pretoria (administrative) and Johannesburg (commercial). Further to the South-East coal was discovered in sufficiently large quantities to power Eskom's electrical generation and for 67 million tons/year to be exported, some half of it to Asia.

The Australian Climate Commission says that if we go on burning coal as we are, many unprecedented climate changes will be so severe that our society will cease to exist as we know it today. Many of the climate change risks that scientists warned of years ago are now happening. The Australian report entitled *"The Critical Decade"* states unequivocally *"that most fossil fuels must be left in the ground."* Even the British Meteorological Office is warning of wet summer weather for up to a decade. Britain experienced the coldest December in 100 years in 2010, followed by the second wettest summer on record in 2012 and the coldest spring for 50 years in 2013. The North Atlantic has become warmer and the high-altitude jet stream above it has drifted south.

The response of the South African Police Service to those who protested against President Obama visiting the country was… guess what? …Stun grenades! After Marikana, SKY Correspondent Alex Crawford asked, *"Has South Africa learned nothing in the last 40 years?"* I now think that there was a prophetic message in the words that are ringing in my ears. I had a sheet of paper and a biro beside me when I watched news bulletins on a couple of channels in the aftermath of the massacre that shocked me profoundly. The last 'horror' that I had seen on TV was when I walked into Christina McKenzie's kitchen in Haselbech, Northamptonshire, with the morning paper that I had collected whilst walking the dogs. There was a film on about aeroplanes flying into skyscrapers and exploding. 'Film' my eye, I realised as the Twin Towers crumbled and I found my hostess transfixed by what she saw on her library television set. 9/11 was a sad morning for America.

On my blank sheet of paper, the reverse side of part of our Telkom bill, I noted from a series of SABC and SKY News bulletins some salient points, many of which will probably have been addressed before the Commission of Inquiry which, of course at that time had not been called. The points noted were:

- Rubber bullets fired at the worker's shacks to flush out men wanted by SAPS,
- Arbitrary punishment by SAPS against the mining community,
- Praying at the Community Hall placing hope in God,
- No income paid to striking miners for 6 weeks,
- Miners betrayed by bosses, unions and government.
- Rock-drill operators have been trying to get improved pay.
- Miners paid R4,000/month to extract metal (platinum) for cars and jewellery.
- On 13th August, the delegation wanted more miners to join.
- "We don't want to kill policemen."
- 16th was D-Day as far as police were concerned.
- The miners on the koppie were waiting for their leaders to address them about wages.
- Fewer than a dozen killed in the TV news clip. The rest were killed on the koppie where they hid.
- Thapelo Lekgowa (interviewed) knew nothing of small koppie.
- Miners shot at spots marked with yellow letters on bare rocks.
- The geography of the place ruled out anything except premeditated murder.
- 'N' was killed at close range. The story was published a week later.
- A miner was shot in the hand as he put it up to surrender and was shot in the stomach for a 2nd time.
- Man shot in the head whilst trying to surrender. RFD-tv saw police shooting men who were trying to surrender.
- Video sound recording of police bragging about taking people out with a gun vs. R4 rifle.
- A week later the original yellow letters were defaced to forestall speculation or cover-up.
- Why were yellow markings changed by defacing – Centre for Applied Legal Studies –
    - Not a single police officer suspended.

- Force used to resolve mining problems.
- What happened away from the cameras?
- Need to name every operational police officer.
- T.V. viewers not clear as to why the miners were shot at.

Marikana might not have happened in such a fatal and serious manner for the country. The ZAR:US$ stood @ 8.23; R12.95:£1 and R10.17:€1. Gold stood @ $1604.5/oz. and platinum @ $1,400. Ten months later the rates are 9.93 (-17.1); 15.57 (-16.8) and 13.2 (-22.9) and the largest fall is against the currency of Europe, a principle trading partner. This may help some exports. Gold has fallen 13.6% and platinum has gained 4.3%.

One of the first statements made by NEW AGE *News* following the tragic massacre by police simply says, *"Thousands of strikers began leaving the rocky outcrop they had occupied when they saw heavily armed officers laying out barbed wire barricades."* Reuters reporter Poloku Tau may have hit the nail right on the head – bang!

The containment of a crowd is called Kettling. It is an exercise that dates right back to the Battle of Thermopylae, 480 B.C., when a small army of some 6,300 Spartans and Greeks from city-states under the Spartan King Leonidas defended a narrow mountain pass to thwart the invasion by 100,000 men under the Persian Emperor Xerxes. The Persians could not force their way over a wall that blocked the pass. A Greek traitor revealed the existence of a little-known alternative route. This enabled the best soldiers of the Persian army to encircle and 'kettle' the Greeks in the pass and defeat them, the Spartans fighting to the last. The Zulu army 'kettled' the 24th Regiment of the British Army at Isandlwana (1879) and containment by 'kettling' has become the international norm for police forces controlling large crowds. When executed, large cordons of police officers move to contain a crowd within a limited area. This is easiest done where streets can be closed off in urban areas and protesters are confined to an area such as Parliament Square, London; Place de la Concorde, Paris; or Tahrir Square, Cairo where every policeman wore a protective helmet and carried long batons and riot shields. Officers performing riot control typically wear protective equipment such as riot helmets, face visors, body armour, gas masks and riot shields –

not in South Africa they don't!

When the cordon is set up protesters are left with just one or two choices of exit, as determined by the police. They can be prevented from leaving for several hours, identified and disarmed as they pass through a barrier. Crowd Control precedes Riot Control. It calls for gentler tactics and it is essential to keep a crowd comfortable and relaxed. Strikers on the koppie at Marikana were awaiting news of negotiations by union representatives with Lonmin, the employer, when the police commenced slowly preparing to kettle them.

Where a riot situation occurs, police, military and other security forces (anywhere except South Africa) use batons, whips, teargas, pepper spray, rubber bullets and electric tasers. In some cases riot squads may also use long-range acoustic devices, water cannon, armoured fighting vehicles, police dogs or police mounted on horses. In many countries it is illegal to use lethal force to control riots in all but the most extreme circumstances. Non-lethal riot-control tools are lachrymatory agents such as pepper spray (active ingredient: capsaicin) and various kinds of tear gas. They can rapidly produce sensory irritation or disabling physical effects which usually disappear within 15 minutes for tear gas, or up to 2 hours for pepper spray.) SAPS special force at Marikana had more live ammunition than disabling equipment so they used it randomly.

The instances where lethal weapons have recently been used have been confined to the venues of the Arab Spring such as Cairo, Alexandria, Libya and now Syria. Earlier scenes were the 1956 Hungarian Revolution, Tiananmen Square and of course Soweto.

Kevin Sutherland's photo in the Durban *Mercury* the day after the Marikana massacre shows approximately 12 out of 25 officers in one frame wearing helmets with visors. Police had known for five days before the fatal event that general dealer, Mohammed Cassim, had run out of pangas following 30 being sold in just a few days. Nobody is disputing the fact that many miners acted illegally and had no right to turn on Warrant Officers Tsietsi Monene and S.R. Lepaaku and hack them to death. Such action is the nemesis of pent-up frustration and desire to change things for the better. The Farlam Inquiry will fathom why they were there at the time, whoever sent them and what their objective was. Not giving them covering support may be found to have been crass negligence.

A further photograph by Phil Magakoe shows two of eight officers with helmets. Felix Dlangamandla captured shots of strikers chanting war songs and brandishing weapons in an intimidating manner. Whoever tipped off these good photographers to the effect that a nasty situation was imminent and that they might get some good photos, also knew of the threat faced and that soft berets and uniform caps were little protection against the pangas and traditional sticks of the strikers. What seems much more important for Judge Farlam to fathom and report on is what had been going on for a long time in the 'turf' war between the National Union of Miners and the Association of Mineworkers and Construction Union representatives over union membership and how Lonmin responded to reports from Union representatives meeting Management.

Before one loses sight of the nature of the tragic event, let us return a moment to kettling. Photos thereof show just a small minority of police officers wearing helmets. The majority wore soft berets. There is not a water cannon to be seen. There is not a riot shield in sight. There are no police dogs or mounted police. Large numbers of police or military personnel are required to effectively cordon a large crowd. It was known that thousands were on the koppie whereas just 761 officers were deployed. Strikers awaited union representatives coming to tell them about wage negotiations and then they could return to their shacks and prepare for a return to work on the next shift if all was agreed.

Wire can be deployed at a rate of 100m/min by two men. Mobile security concertina wire is intended to provide quick protection and on level ground may be deployed at a fast rate three tiers high from a moving vehicle. It may also be easily recovered, though at three times slower a pace. The equipment must be kept out of sight of protesters or rioters until the last moment. Intentionally-made gaps must be manned at all times. On the day of the massacre, Kevin Sutherland captured a picture of a long two-wheeled trailer towed by a police vehicle preparing to release six rolls of coiled barbed wire to make a cordon about 2.5m high. They were watched by an audience of hundreds of strikers.

Rule 1 of Kettling: **Don't let the intended victims know that you are about to encircle them!**

It will no doubt register on the Farlam Inquiry that the political appointments of Jackie Selebi (by President Mbeki) and Bheki Cele (by President Zuma) were two for the most disastrous appointments made by post-apartheid ANC Presidents. Neither appears to have had the faintest clue about policing and changed things like ranks (civil to military) simply to militarise a civilian force of law and order. Both appointees were up to their necks in corruption and had no time for proper administration of this vital law-keeping civilian service. Transforming a Station Commander into a Colonel does not change his job or make the service any more efficient. Ms Sorry! General Riah Phiyega had been 10 weeks in the job before Marikana. As Police Commissioner, the dame is in the firing line and she has had a hard time justifying the actions by the police at the Inquiry. The General has not spent a day of her life in any service institution. If sitting on the board that applied to hold the FIFA World Cup in South Africa, working as an 'executive' at ABSA or doing a stint with Transnet are necessary qualifications for a national police commissioner then, as the Germans say, "*Rumpelstilzchen ist mein namen!*" Good governance includes putting the right people in the right job. The world is watching and it is hoped that President Obama's voice is not alone in rooting for South Africa's success when America is willing to offer so much help with the development and aspirations of present university students.

Whatever is known, or not known in South Africa about international police tactics and kettling, is not as important as the fact that application of the tactic here was weak in the extreme. Failure to properly deploy the wire in quick time led to a rush of watching strikers desiring to escape the possibility of being encircled. Command is always at the heart of such incidents. If those in command do not have the training, experience and expertise the winner is nearly always the one who makes the least mistakes, as in war. The chain of command goes to the top. Training remains on the ground. SAPS officers have been to Britain and other countries. British officers have visited South Africa on training missions. After a taxi industry turf war on the outskirts of Durban in early 2013, a police officer was seen on SABC 3 national evening news to pick up with a bare hand a discarded hand gun that had just been used in a crime. That police officer's fingerprints compromise the evidence of gun ownership. When evidence is collected under such circumstances, gloves must be worn. Police officers I have spoken with know that. The officer probably knew it too but never thought his action would be on that evening's news. Does the mistake by the officer lie with him personally or with his superior? The National Police Commissioner passes suitable names to the Office of the President for selection of the top police appointment by the President. This is where the ultimate safety and security of the people of the republic rests. Photographs of those they serve adorn every police station. The precedent of two bungling criminals (Selebi and Cele) did not augur well for the present female incumbent. SAPS accepts its role as custodian of law and order. A force devoid of good leadership and subjected to role and rank changes may be forgiven for being confused and un-coordinated.

In the immediate aftermath of the bloodbath leaders of the NUM and AMCU outright condemned the police for killing so many of their members. Finding out later that many had been shot in the back or whilst surrendering exacerbated the situation. Taking into consideration that the strikers were waiting for reports of a union meeting with employers (Lonmin), it is no surprise that the employers came under pressure to explain their role. The event occurred as the Chief Executive, Ian Farmer, was being hospitalised back to London with a serious illness. Lonmin's day-to-day business became the responsibility of an executive committee under Roger Phillimore. The shares fell 15% to R83.70, wiping R2bn of the third biggest platinum producer's market value. The violence revealed deep-seated problems in labour relations and the police response showed how ill-prepared the authorities were to deal with the simmering tensions of disgruntled workers demanding more money.

Lonmin, whilst recognising that its 2012 production target of 750,000 ounces of saleable platinum would be missed, was every bit as edgy that its covenants with its bank were likely to be tested. Production ceased for six days two days before 'Marikana' and 15,000oz. of production was lost. No production, no income, no wages. Of the 2.4m tonne drop in mined platinum output for the year, 1.8m.t. (75%) was associated with Marikana. In other areas gold mining shrank 8%, production also being hampered by underground fires. Diamond production fell due to lack of skill in the workforce and lower quality ore.

When President Jacob Zuma attended the annual G20 conference in Davos five months later he told the world that Lonmin was to blame for 'Marikana' for having negotiated with some workers outside the formal bargaining system, thus causing excluded workers to resort to wildcat strikes. President Zuma set up the Commission whose duty it is to report what Judge Farlam and his Senior Counsel colleagues find. For a country's President to forestall the outcome of his appointed Commission almost a year before it was due to report must surely be without legal precedent. *Sunday Times* (30/6/13) reporters Jackie Dugard and Kate Tissington suggested that the Inquiry was going so slowly that it was *"hearing barely one witness a month and must complete its work by the end of October."* They suggest that the Commission's proceedings need curtailing and that the Inquiry needs to focus on the core events at Marikana. Both young ladies are 'long' in socio-economic rights and ex-CALS at Witwatersrand University.

Since 'Marikana' most likely commenced a long time before the massacre near Wonderkop, it would be erroneous not to delve right to the heart of the annual bargaining system and to examine minutes of meetings between employer and employees.

The South African loves to *"move on."* It is a meretricious phrase that gives the user a false feeling of escapism from accountability and responsibility for an occurrence. *"Move on"* is a password to evasiveness from giving any logical reason for any happening, trivial or serious. If, as the young journalists *(above)* suggest, the Farlam Inquiry into 'Marikana' might risk being shelved until after the 2014 election to avoid any Presidential embarrassment, other events will have transpired and there will be a plethora of alternatives to think about. That is not going to be any consolation to the families of the bereaved, injured and wronged. The Inquiry must proceed apace and, for once, give the people of South Africa the truth.

With no apologies for the euphemism, we must move on to the historical background of the people participating in this revolutionary scene, how they have developed through the ages of man and where they fit into C.21st. They have come a long way in 200 years and, as visiting President Obama's countrymen say, they are *"gainin' ground all the time, man"*.

The first anniversary of the massacre of miners fleeing from the prospect of being kettled in a faulty cordon and search plan put into motion by SAPS came and went with much prayer, thought, grievance, anxiety, column inches and photographs plus a documentary that showed only half the truth. A TV documentary on eNCA included footage of a miner in his death throes. The showing of film containing a fatality is prohibited in many parts of the world. This is Africa. His widow was able to see her husband sitting up clutching his right leg then collapsing dead from bullet wounds a few moments later. Executive producer Patrick Conroy gets away with it, eNCA gets away with it in a country where, since the days of Shaka 180 years ago, a life has so little value. One of the greatest current concerns was the matter of funding of the legal representation at the Farlam Commission of Inquiry. They sat again on 19th August 2013.

If a growing gum tree is likely to impede the circular passage of the arm of an irrigation pivot, it is cut down and chopped up. In our case the young tree marked a corner of our smallholding. Good neighbour, Mark Anderson, telephoned to ask if he could please remove the tree to enable his new irrigation pivot to pass. Then he went to Jack Lund at Hazeldene (tree) Nursery and bought us three different coloured liquid-amber type trees to plant by our dam so that they would reflect their colours towards the house. He even gave us three bags of kraal manure to ensure they got a good start when planted. That's good neighbourliness by a man who has lost two sons in the last three years, one in a misadventure with a gun, the second from rabies.

If a farmer has a row with employees and dismisses some without general consultation, he is vulnerable to a revenge attack. One is more likely to be delayed than immediate and that puts inside information and security at a premium. 25.6% of the workforce being unemployed necessitates that criminal activity probably leads to food on the table or beer in the belly. If an elderly couple should impede a burglary for the purpose of acquiring quickly saleable goods and chattels, they can be cut down as easily as a young gum tree.

The eNCA television documentary put together a lot of edited film taken on 16th August 2012. The more one watched it and read articles in the media, the more one's suspicions were aroused that a hidden government agenda could exist to bring the Farlam Inquiry to a conclusion. On television and in the press there were references to the inquiry dragging on. Fresh film of those revisiting the koppie showed a former miner on crutches. He was shot seven times last year yet survived. Anyone thinking that well over a thousand statements and several hours of video footage from a number of sources can be reviewed by a highly competent retired Judge and two Senior Counsel in a matter of months when so many issues were at stake is not living in the real world of South Africa.

Over and over again TV viewers saw a posse of running miners being mown down by police who had been authorised to use lethal methods where Riot Control officers elsewhere have for more than thirty years used tear gas, pepper spray, rubber bullets, electric Tasers, long-range acoustic devices, water cannon, armoured fighting vehicles, police dogs and mounted police of which there were pitifully few present. Frequently the reason given for police resorting to the lethal method is that the miners were heavily armed and had refused to lay down their weapons. It may be said that the use of lethal force prevented any of the 718 policemen receiving a scratch, cut or bruise. What is not so simply explained is the omissions from the television documentary. The words "*No cameras,*" are heard not long after *Cease fire!* Without having been there on the ground last year it is not possible to translate these orders by a police officer simply. Only hindsight gives one an inkling that a follow-up might have been mooted in a police brief. The cameramen in helicopters got the best view of what followed. If, say 16 miners, lay dead, dying or wounded after the gunfire on the flat, how is the figure 34 arrived at? The inquiry will no doubt reveal exact figures notwithstanding the fact that the evidence recorded on the koppie was tampered with. It seems reasonably safe to assume that what took place in front of the media and police cameras may best be described as 'Episode 1'. In the subsequent episode police followed fleeing miners towards the koppie and summarily executed a further 18, shooting many of them in the back. This brings to the fore the fact that if the police force as a whole is 'militarised' a special section is trained to do the job of the army. Currently (mid-August), the residents of Manenberg are asking for the army to be called in to quell gang violence affecting schools. Manenberg is a township of Cape Town that was created by the apartheid government for low-income coloured families in the Cape Flats. It has an estimated population of 70,000 residents. In Northern Ireland '1 Para' did the job of a militarised police unit on Bloody Sunday (30th January 1972) when 26 unarmed civil rights protesters were shot by soldiers. Thirteen were killed, and five of the wounded were shot in the back. After publication of a report in 2010, British Premier David Cameron made a formal apology which greatly facilitated Queen Elizabeth II having such a successful reconciliation visit to the Republic of Ireland the following year. It was the first visit by a reigning monarch to the Republic. King George V and Queen Mary had visited in 1911.

Military forces in Egypt are doing the same job now in Cairo and Alexandria. There is talk of the Muslim Brotherhood being outlawed as a political force. It should be remembered that the Irish Republican Brotherhood was a forerunner to Sinn Féin and the Provisional IRA. Religion has festered more conflict between ethnic groups than any other factor including land. For all the lives lost in two world wars, precious little land has changed hands. Yes, Germany lost territories in Africa at Versailles after WW1 (Namibia was German West Africa. Burundi, Rwanda and Tanganyika were East African colonies. Parts of the Cameroon, Nigeria, Chad, Gabon, the Congo, Central African Republic and Tonga were also 'confiscated' as a result of 19-year-old Serbian student, Gavrito Prinzip, assassinating Archduke Franz Ferdinand of Austria on a street corner in Sarajevo on 28th June 1914. Was the blood-soaked soil of the Somme, Delville Wood, North-West Europe, Italy, France, Belgium, the Netherlands, Burma and Indonesia really worth the acres of foreign soil that changed ownership? I have a 'Kennedy' uncle who was killed when commanding 3 Company, 1st Bn. Irish Guards on his 13th time in action, just inside Germany from Holland. It was the last battalion engagement of WW2 visited at Millsbeck military cemetery near Venlo. He won a Military Cross at Anzio, Italy in 1943. A rare tribute to his life entitled *'Major D.M. (John) Kennedy. M.C.'* was written half a century later by his nephew Robert Jocelyn. Few books exist about the whole lives of WW2 army officers who were killed in action. Many Irish, and South African, lives were given to the Allied cause to defeat the Nazis in Europe and the Japanese in the Far East.

Michael McGillycuddy was awarded a Military Medal for his part as a Field Security Policeman at Willems, in the evacuation of Dunkirk with Field Security Police. Later in Burma he was awarded an 'Immediate' Military Cross for his conspicuous gallantry and devotion to duty at Pineblu with the Chindits. He features significantly in John Masters' *'The Road Past Mandalay'* (See p. 164).

He lies in grave 4, Row K, Plot 13, Taukkyan cemetery, Rangoon. My McGillycuddy grandfather, who gained a D.S.O. and Croix de Guerre in WW1, rejoined the Colours aged 57 in 1939, followed by all four of his children. John joined the 2nd Bn. Northamptonshire Yeomanry, Dermot, the Royal Air Force Volunteer Reserve (Fighter Command), Michael transferred, via Sandhurst, to his father's 4/7th Royal Dragoon Guards then to 3/4th PWO Gurkhas, and Phyllida to A.P.S., North Africa, as an ambulance driver (Army No. 97080).

It remains to be seen what improvement arises in the miners' lot and industrial relations in that industry. The 44 lives lost around Marikana need 'paying for'. One big difference between those lost in war and in civil conflict – the miners were killed by fellow countrymen in a civil war manifested out of a steady social revolution.

It was unsettling to learn that funding of the representation of the families of the deceased was in jeopardy. The inquiry sat again on 19th August with the issue seemingly resolved. If someone set a 'cap' on the matter, they failed utterly to take into consideration the complexity of requiring the Commission of Inquiry to report so much. If the Inquiry had stalled, South Africa would be on the rocks like coasters hugging the shore and grounding. The Human Rights Commission should ensure that the government does not shirk the issue. The Constitution guaranteed dignity, life, freedom and safety in 1996. Its failure is deplorable – worthy of the description, 'odious nation'.

Marikana: SAPS the big loser
Marikana: Where is the justice?
Farlam report blames Marikana victims

read the news headlines when Judge Farlam's Commission reported at the end of June 2015, nearly three years after the massacre. As long anticipated, the National Police Commissioner, Major General Riah Phiyega, bore the brunt of criticism in the Commission's 600-page report read by President Zuma. Deputy President Cyril Ramaphosa, and other Ministers got off Scot-free. [Incidentally this term originates in the name of a Scandinavian tax, or 'Scat'. It later had a Scottish connotation when the Scots were supposed to pay a C.12th municipal tax and some did not. The term has nothing to do with the late Jeremy Thorpe, M.P., and leader of the Liberal Party walking Scott-free from the Old Bailey in 1979 after being acquitted of arranging the killing of his homosexual friend Norman Scott.] The Deputy President was alleged by Counsel for the injured and arrested people to have been the cause of the massacre. The Farlam Commission found the allegation groundless. Some of the blame for Marikana was attributable to Lonmin and the two mining unions involved.

The Police Service was the big loser. They were caught out over the timing of management decision-making regarding the prospective kettling and tactical operations. Senior Counsel led evidence voluntarily submitted by this writer as to how kettling should have been implemented before resort to a tactical firearms operation. The miners were seeking to escape the possibility of being cordoned and forced to lay down their arms when the police opened fire and 34 deaths occurred. On that fateful August 16th police management abandoned the decision to cordon off the miners. The Commission was told that the decision had been taken the previous day. The Commission found that it would have been impossible to disarm the striking miners and disperse them without "significant bloodshed". The decision to use firearms (tactical operation) was taken by police management and not by the police facing the miners on the ground.

Lonmin was the next corporate institution to be fingered by Judge Farlam. It was found that the international mining company had not used its best endeavours to resolve the industrial dispute. The company had not responded appropriately to the threat of and the outbreak of violence.

The Association of Mineworkers and Construction Union (AMCU) had not exercised effective control over its members and supporters. The National Union of Mineworkers (NUM) was rapped over the knuckles for not effectively dealing with a dispute between the union and the striking workers. Both AMCU and NUM were said to have failed to control their members. NUM wrongly advised rock drill operators that no negotiations with Lonmin were possible until the end of the two-year wage agreement. The Union had not taken the initiative to persuade Lonmin to speak to the workers.

The Commission recommended a full investigation under the Director of Public Prosecutions (North-West) with a view to ascertaining criminal liability on the part of all members of the Police Service who were involved in the incidents. The investigation team should be headed by a Senior State Advocate, with independent experts in the reconstruction of crime scenes, expert ballistic and forensic pathologists and others of this calibre as necessary. The prescripts on public order policing and the adequacy of the training of police with specialised equipment such as water cannon and video equipment should also be reviewed. On December 12th, 2016, the National Prosecuting Service said that they were still working on gathering evidence regarding top police officers that could be charged regarding the massacre well over four years ago. They still are! (at 20/02/2017).

CHAPTER II

HISTORY

Henry Fynn

Fynn (b. 1803) left England aged 15 and arrived in the Cape of Good Hope in 1818 and headed for Somerset Farm, the home of Lord Charles Somerset, Governor of Cape Colony. The farm lay at the foot of the Boschberg mountains somewhere between the Great Fish and Little Fish Rivers that flow through the Garden Route north of Grahamstown. The latter river flowed through the farm. It came under the management of former Cape Corps Adjutant, Robert Hart, in 1817 and fulfilled the role of purchasing cattle, sheep and corn from the Boers. These were later sent on with Hottentot herdsmen and wagon drivers to the military outposts of the colony. Kaffirs (we're not allowed to call them that now!) had been raiding within the colony border and it was necessary for all consignments to be accompanied by military escorts. The area became more secure with the arrival of the Albany Settlers. These were 66 parties of people mostly from England who settled in the Albany district, some of it now being the Addo Elephant National Park.

Fynn left the farm in 1822 and walked the 700km ('as the crow flies') to Cape Town. Few of his age (19) today can walk 700m without a cell phone call or text message! His feat was an outstanding manifestation of the character of the people that made South Africa. One of the first people he met there was Henry Nourse whom he had previously met on the Frontier. Fynn's brother William was employed by ship's chandler, John Murray, and he went to stay with him. Despairing of finding suitable employment (he was a little too proud to ask), he contemplated return to England but there were no ships going that way. One day his brother heard in the chandlery that a brig called the *Mary* and a sloop, the *Jane,* were about to be sent on a trading mission to Delagoa Bay, now Maputo in Portuguese Mozambique.

Mr Nourse's nephew, Henry Maynard, was appointed cargo master for the *Mary* and Fynn took that role on the *Jane*. He joined his ship in Simon's Town, a naval base then under the command of Joseph Nourse, brother of the chandler (how times have not changed!). At this same time Royal Navy Lieutenants Farewell and Saunders-King were preparing for a voyage along the African-Indian coast to St. Lucia Bay which, unknown to them, was to have deep ramifications. The voyage under a frequently intoxicated Captain Fotheringham was to take 12 days of June 1824 and they were fortunate in encountering little severe Indian Ocean weather in mid-winter. Off St. Lucia they found themselves surrounded by five waterspouts, two of which swiftly approached the ship and might have engulfed her.

A small cannon was heavily charged and fired at the two waterspouts, causing their dissipation. A waterspout is a gyrating column of mist, spray and water produced by a whirlwind, as with a 'Twister' on land.

When the intoxicated Captain Fotheringham ran the stern of the sloop onto the bank of Elephant Island and endangered the vessel, he was relieved of his command and the Cape Commodore's Coxwain, William Collins took command. The sloop was thrown on her beam ends, the cargo shifted and several of the crew fell overboard into shallow water. With the assistance of a whaler, the *Saucy Jack,* and the turn of the tide, all who had been sitting on the keel for extra ballast, climbed back on board as the ship righted and was subsequently anchored in the Mbuluzi River (formerly St. George's River) opposite the Portuguese fort on the north side. They were now on the Tembe side which was under Chief Mayetha. 42km to the south now lies Bela Vista and Maputo Elephant Reserve, one each side of the Maputo River running north. Beyond this lay the amaThonga tribe under Chief Maklasana.

The ship's manifest was submitted to the Portuguese Governor who expressed a strong desire to purchase the entire cargo wholesale, contrary to the intention of the owners. Fynn awaited the arrival of the *Mary* a few days later followed by the armed sloop *Leven* and her consort, the *Barracota*, who anchored in the mouth of the river. It was September, 1822. The ships were respectively under the command of Captain Vidal, and the *Cockburn* was under Lieutenant R. Owen. They were under the supreme command of Captain W.F.W. Owen, who to Fynn resembled the Elizabethan Admiral Drake.

The original Portuguese fort of Maputo, dating back to about 1764, was built of mud walls with 8 to 10 very rusty cannons. Mr Collins commented that it would probably be safer to be in front of them than behind when they were fired. In the cells below the chapel were about 80 slaves in irons, the booty of inter-tribal rivalry having led to their purchase by the Portuguese. Remember; this was just 190 years ago. The earliest settlers of Maputo were a Governor, a few sub-officers, a priest who held services in the 12sq. ft. chapel, 5 or 6 licensed traders of Portuguese extraction and a number of dark skinned natives collected locally and drilled on military lines. On gala days the officers wore the most dashing uniforms they possessed but the natives lacked jackets and shoes. The principal provisions were fowl, pigs, eggs and rice which was grown locally in large quantities by the natives. The soldiers reared most of their own provisions. Fish was abundant as may be expected, the natives using reed fences on poles as standing nets.

The desire to acquire elephant tusks directly from the native population up the Maputo River necessitated taking the *Mary* inland, accompanied by the Reverend William Trefall. This gentleman of the cloth had previously been here under Captain Owen who had contemplated the Tembe country south of the port being ceded to Great Britain, but without success. As they were crossing the bay prior to their departure a hippopotamus rose out of the water near the sloop. Men watching from the *Leven* took to a boat armed with harpoons and set off after it. Whilst many were looking over one side, the hippo came up the other side, gripped the gunwale in its jaws and tore out the side of the boat. The sailors had to swim for it and were rescued by the *Mary* and put back on their own ship. The hippo is responsible for more human fatalities in Africa than any other large animal. Male hippos actively defend their territories which run along the banks of rivers and lakes. Females have also been known to get extremely aggressive if they sense anyone coming in between their babies, who stay in the water while she feeds on the shore. Hippos can run at speeds of over 20 miles an hour and they have enormous jaws which host up to 20-inch canines.

It took three days to go 40 miles upstream, taking numerous soundings as they left the sea for fresh water. They met a number of natives who lived in the densely covered beautiful forestry along the banks. The natives sailed boats resembling the Indian Massuly boats. They made swift trades until interrupted by the Portuguese. It should be remembered that the English and the Portuguese are Europe's oldest allies.

Fynn encountered Orontont natives who belonged to the Zulu main tribe. They were feared by the natives of Delagoa Bay and some could speak English. A party of them accompanied Fynn to a native kraal and in the course of conversation he learned that their chief was King Shaka who resided at not too great a distance. At this point the fever struck Fynn and he was ill for several days. A native doctor and some women buried him upright for about half an hour up to his neck in a hot pit that they had dug and warmed with a fire at the bottom. They then carried him back to his hut where native medicine was administered. By the third day of his recovery he was again able to communicate with the *Mary*.

Put into timely (2014) perspective, this event occurred just 190 years ago. In England Lord Byron died, in France Louis XVIII died, all was quiet in Prussia but not in the Cape colony where the Kaffirs created problems. Lord Combermere (as in Combermere Barracks, Windsor) commanded in India, and in Burma the British took Rangoon and purchased Singapore. In Ireland, Daniel O'Connell worked tirelessly towards 'Liberation' of the Catholics.

Fynn had earlier sailed the small (c. 25 ton) sloop Julia in the autumn of 1824 into what we now know as Durban Port, they anchored where the Custom House now stands. The ship's boat took him and three others and their provisions ashore. The three 'mechanics' (builders) were to build the first house of Durban on Kangela Flat. After a long walk on the beach seeking inhabitants, they slept in the open until woken about midnight by a violent rainstorm. Their bedding became drenched and they moved out of their sheltered hollow to avoid the sudden flow into it of a stream of rainwater. They had collected plenty of firewood and had a good fire going. Whilst doing their best to keep warm and get dry again they realised that they were surrounded by howling 'wolves' – actually spotted hyæna (*Crocuta crocuta*). In defiance of their shouts and a blazing fire, the hyaena approached nearer and nearer from the pitch dark. The four men stood back-to-back brandishing burning log ends with which a few of the beasts were struck. One hyaena seized from their abandoned bedding a pair of leather trousers which had a Dutch 60-dollar note in the pocket. Ogle, the English owner, rushed forward, grabbed the band of his trousers and succeeded in recovering them, minus one leg which the predator ripped off.

Once sufficient daylight came they hailed the sloop's boat and returned to the *Julia* for breakfast and to recount their experience. Later they set off for Cato's Creek where the Durban Town Hall now stands. The story illustrates one small experience less than two centuries ago. Has any race become upgraded as fast as the South Africans? Is it a surprise to anyone that having moved so fast in 200 years some detail should have been skipped? If they capitalise as fast upon the experiences of other nations over the next 200 years, where will they be in 2214? That's revolution for you. Bloodless? I wonder.

CHAPTER III

SHAKA

The revered creator of the Zulu nation, from a number of insignificant smaller tribes, was the ruthless King Shaka. He possessed political ambition, military flair and macabre cruelty, traits for which he became greatly respected by his people regardless of what cruelty he inflicted. Henry Fynn found the extremes of his character part of his natural make-up. Whilst writing his book in about 1934, Dr Bryant described him as the Hitler of his time, such was already the reputation of the new German Chancellor. This comment from the depths of South Africa on a relatively new European political leader might well have been provoked by news reaching German West Africa (Namibia since 1990) that 25,000 books were thrown onto a bonfire in Berlin in the first of the Nazis' book burnings. When Shaka was visited early in the day at his Bulawayo kraal, between Eshowe and Empangeni, he was found in his bath and, being on the Pompeian model, anyone could walk in. Three page boys were in attendance, two carrying gourds of water, and the third a black dish. The king soaped himself with a paste of bruised fat and ground Kaffir-corn. His valet washed the parts of his majesty's back that he could not reach, being somewhat portly, with Kwezo leaves. He chatted with his audience then suddenly ordered one of the men nearby off to instant execution (by strangulation) for no reason that Doctor Bryant and his missionaries could find. It was to become a common occurrence during the day. As the king dried off in the warm air, a bearer of cosmetics, arms outstretched as is Zulu etiquette when offering or receiving anything from a superior. The king applied a lump of red clay paste to his skin, rubbing the mixture well in. The habit was found amongst the early Egyptians and continues amongst the natives to this day. Finally some sheep-tail fat or Native butter gave the skin a ruddy silky gloss befitting his position as leader. Shaka dressed into a brown-black kilt of furry tails with armlets, leglets and pieces of hair from cows' tails in a manner that is regularly seen now on frequent ceremonial occasions. Seated on his chair or a roll of inDulirushes, his head and body were bedecked with red plumes from the Lowrie bird and variegated beadwork, coloured beads always having great decorative attraction as featured on the current national Standard Postage stamps from the Ndebele-iziko collection. When the king required the presence of an official or servant, the man was sent for by one of the king's 'sisters' or had his name bellowed across the palisade of the kraal. Replying Nkozi (Sire!) and arriving a safe distance from the king's hut, the summoned person raised his right hand above his head in salute, shouting Nkosi again followed by a string of praise-names in adulation. Moving into the king's presence the person half-reclined, left hip and elbow on the floor to receive his orders, accepting them with further Nkosis or Baba (father). He would finally crawl back out the small doorway of the hut.

Court etiquette was more in keeping with cavemen than the bows and curtseys expected in the presence of umGeorge, as this King came to know the English monarch from Fynn's descriptions. King George IV reigned for the decade 1820-1830. Going to war was not done without invoking the aid of magic and of the gods. Medicinal fortification was in practice long before Shaka and continues to this day. One asks what is it that hunting people take from a stirrup cup at a meet before setting off on the chase? A Sangoma (witch doctor) played a significant part in bolstering the morale of striking miners on the koppe at Marikana in case they should need protection against the police. The application of medicine would enable them to ward off the effect of bullets. Well it may have worked for some but not for the 34 who were massacred, or wounded on 16th August 2012. Briefly, the medicine man treated warriors as follows. He held in his hand an isiNdwili bulb and thrust it in the face of each man, asking, "Do you see him?" The answer was always, "Yebo!" Next, a wartorch of fiercely blazing grass was taken around the circle of men touching them on the bare chest and ribs. If a man should feel burned, the doctor would pronounce him as containing bad medicine. The Sangoma laid aside the burning grass and smeared each man fore and aft, and his weapons with inTelezl sprinkled on as a war charm. The red roots of the uMobopd tree (Moth Fruit) (*Acridocarpus natalitius*) were an invariable ingredient. The slippery substance would protect the warriors against dangers such as enemy assegais which would slip harmlessly away leaving the body uninjured. Courage and tenacity was imbued by each warrior biting of the end of the end of a cooked strip of beef, chewing on it to extract the potent medicines that it contained and swallowing the remains. After biting off his piece the warrior threw the strip into the air for the next man to catch as if it was a flung snake. Where Oliver Cromwell's Ironside Puritan troops of the English Civil War preached Trust in God, they actually placed far greater emphasis upon keeping dry the powder used in their muskets in the wet English climate. The Zulu placed his faith in the tribal gods, none other than the ancestors for whom he had the greatest respect, to see them to victory. Shaka brought the Zulu people from being bands of small family clans to an army comprising 10 to 15 thousand soldiers divided into about half a dozen regiments. Just as the migration of the Bantu people appears to have been three pronged, coastal, inland and central, so was the advance of the British Army across Zululand under General Thesiger, later Lord Chelmsford, before the fateful battle of Isandlwana on 21st January 1879. One column was to go up the coastal region, one through the centre and one through the western part of Zululand. The Zulu army was likewise divided into three main divisions; isitba was the central core containing the older regiments of warriors wearing head rings (isiCoco), carrying white shields and who bore the brunt of the head-to-head clash; isimPondo was the term applied to the flanks, or horns (as in buffalo), that were trained to encircle the enemy. Their warriors carried dark hide shields and did not wear headbands. From the horns, parties of warriors (iznlola) were despatched to perfect the encirclement, cutting off any possible retreat.

Head rings came from Swaziland about the time of Shaka's father, Senzangakona. They were not known to the Xhosas of the Cape who had separated from the Zulus about 1600 AD. The head ring was made to fit in a thick 'rope' of palm-fibres and attached to the hair with thread. uNgiyone, the substance taken from branches of bushes where flying insects formed as larvae and chewed in the mouth until it became a gummy substance, was applied to the ring. After hardening the black latex was rubbed with grease then polished with a small pebble, or with the stone-like root of the isiDwo gladiolus, until it acquired the gloss and appearance of black ebony. Both *Gladiolus sericeovillosus* and *watsonius* are extant through Zululand. They are pollinated by bees and were used as a fertility charm for good harvest and in traditional medicine to treat dysentery, sprains, swollen joints, menstrual pain, sterility, and to expel afterbirth. Shaka substituted the heavy bladed spear called an assegai for the old javelin, although this was still carried in case of need. The assegai was deemed preferential at close quarters. An ox hide shield was carried on the left arm, a few assegais being held in that hand. Every army has its scouts and sends out patrols to spy out the land and movements of the enemy.

When Chiefs Shaka or Dingane found fault with a report for its inaccuracy they would relieve the unfortunate spy of his eyes, describing them as useless organs and a public danger. The Zulu army also marched on its stomach, living on the land, every man taking as a precaution a skin sack probably containing cooked cow's liver and maize. In battle, the warriors paired off with opponents or fought in small parties/sections.

Having slain his opponent, the Zulu warrior immediately ripped open the abdomen to prevent it swelling in the heat of the day. The custom was directly related to the Zulu view of the afterlife and its relationship with the world of the living. The stomach of the slain enemy was slit open and under the African sun any corpse would quickly putrefy and the gases given off by the early stage of decay cause the stomach to swell. In Zulu belief, this was the soul of the dead warrior vainly trying to escape to the afterlife. The victor was obliged to open the stomach of his victim to allow the spirit to escape, failing which the victor would be haunted by the ghost of his victim who would inflict unmentionable horrors upon him, including causing his own stomach to swell until, eventually, the victor went mad.

CHAPTER IV

CIVIL WAR

It is usually difficult to define the starting point of a civil war. Between 1640 and 1909, revolutions took place in 24 countries. During this period major civil wars took place principally in England, France, the U.S.A. and Chile, a country that seems to have been perpetually at war with itself, its neighbours, or Spain.

Dealing with those we know most about, it was 15 years into his reign that Charles I came to dispute with parliament some of their actions. It followed the Tudor and Elizabethan eras of great glory. The Church of England was re-established with the accession of Elizabeth in 1558. The Spanish Armada was repulsed in 1588, James I came to the throne in 1603 and there was an attempt which we celebrate annually to blow up parliament. Guy Faux is remembered most for having been caught laying the train of fuses on behalf of Catholics dissatisfied with suppression of their faith. A political wag once said that Guy Faux was the only person ever to enter parliament with good intentions! Shakespeare died in 1616 and Sir Walter Raleigh brought tobacco to his Queen (Elizabeth I) on 27th July, 1586, during one of his famous voyages. He appears to be falsely credited with importing the potato. It is more likely to have come to Ireland from Spain when Raleigh was Mayor of Youghal. He was executed in 1618 for having plotted to make Arabella Stuart sovereign of England in place of King James.

Despite the Royalists defeating the Parliamentarians by 12 battles to 8 with 2 drawn, the defeat of Charles II by Oliver Cromwell at Worcester in 1651 was the defining result in favour of the latter named revolutionary. His father had become the first English monarch to be tried and executed in Whitehall on 30th January, 1649.

Cromwell defined himself as Protector of the Commonwealth four years later, holding the position until his death in 1658. His son succeeded him but and resigned eight months later. Royalist General Monk was most influential in securing the restoration of the Monarchy under Charles II a year later in 1660. The English throne has been occupied by a Monarch ever since. Queen Elizabeth II is the Head of State of Great Britain supported by a Prime Minister who is leader of the Conservative and Unionist Party. An Upper House of Peers of the Realm vets proposed legislation (Bill) before returning it with amendments for implementation by parliament before the Bill becomes an Act, being given the Queen's Royal Assent (promulgation). Queen Elizabeth II is the longest ever reigning monarch.

It is sufficient to say that for hundreds of years the Irish suffered the oppression of Imperial forces, a matter that was exacerbated mid-term by the early C.17th plantation of the northern province of Ulster by Scottish Presbyterians and retiring soldiers who had served the Monarch well. The Irish rose against Imperialist domination on Easter Monday 1916 just as many in the sporting world of the Pale was attending Fairyhouse races. The rising was contained by occupying British forces. Some 3,400 people were arrested, more than half of them being interned in England and Wales where they plotted fresh onslaughts on British rule. Fifteen of the leaders were executed. Three years later the Irish Republican Army commenced a guerrilla campaign and by 1920 there were about 20,000 regular British soldiers in Ireland as well as 11,000 police. By the end of 1921 a Treaty was signed in London giving Ireland self-governing dominion of the same constitutional status as Canada. Following a general election the next year the country became divided between the Government who accepted the Treaty and the Republicans who were opposed to Dominion status. A year later a cease fire was declared by Fianna Fail leader Eamon De Valera who had formed the new Republican Party from his Sinn Féin roots. Having won only 35 of the 128 seats in the 1922 general election, Mr De Valera won the 1932 general election and formed a new government. So ended a turbulent period of Irish history, without the issue of the partition of the province of Ulster being resolved. It remains British.

The French Revolution began similarly with the storming of the Bastille on 14th July 1789, a C.14th castle built by King Charles V that had become a State prison. The governor and his officers were captured by the people and their hands and heads were cut off in the Place de Grève, as the inmates were being released. Three years later there was a massacre of 1,200 persons, including 100 priests, in Paris, and a republic was formed by the Convention in September 1792. King Louis XVI was arrested, tried and executed the following January. France, despite being a very divided country had one unifying complaint. The Monarchy had lived exuberantly for too long in a society sorely divided in difference between rich and poor – a common thread between revolutions. When Princess Marie Antoinette was told that the peasants had no bread, she famously replied *"Qu'ils mangent de la brioche."* In translation 'brioche' was taken to mean cake. Think of a flour-based scone and you'll be nearer the mark. Two decades later the Bourbon dynasty was restored and, with the eventual ban of Emperor Napoleon to St. Helena following his defeat by the British at Waterloo (1815), France settled down again. Well, until the Franco-Prussian war commenced in 1870. The guillotine, however, remained in use for capital offences until 1939.

The American Civil War was, and remains, one of the most significant events of the modern world. It was the great point of crisis in the development of the United States, and its repercussions are still felt today. Yet to most people it is a confused collection of political, social and military events, with little pattern behind the differing elements. Leading scholars of American history lay much emphasis on the clash between two fraternal societies, each with sincere but acutely opposed ambitions. The North wished to progress the union of states, the slave-orientated South desired independence. For four years they fought over the most beautiful country on their earth, destroying each other and their homes. Eventually cession of the conflict came in 1865 with the defeat and surrender of the Southern Confederates. From the war arose a hybrid collection of peoples woven into the greatest and most influential nation of the western world.

Revolution is described in the Oxford Dictionary as (2), "Complete change, turning upside-down, great reversal of conditions, fundamental reconstruction, especially forcible substitution by subjects of new ruler, or polity for the old". Hence the conclusion in 1688 of the Stuart dynasty under James II, and the transfer of sovereignty to the Dutch King William III and Queen Mary (the only surviving daughter of James II), when he landed unopposed at

Brixham by invitation of English Protestants on 5th November, 1688. William had ridden to the Protestant cause and defeated the Catholic English King, James II, at the Battle of the Boyne, 1st July, 1690. The defeated monarch later fled from England to France and lived out the rest of his life in exile as a Pretender at a court sponsored by his cousin and ally, King Louis XIV. That was an Anglo-European revolution. The event is commemorated by the Protestants on 12th July, eleven days after the battle date due to changes in the Gregorian calendar made by parliament in 1752.

Civil War is likewise described in terms of the above epoch as a war between members of the same community with emphasis on the struggle between Royalists and Parliament. It may be said that where so many South African civilians are being killed by their own police service, a state of civil war exists. The police have a crisis of their own. Almost every day there is an incident in which the South African Police Service acts in the manner summarised by cartoonist Zapiro. His cartoon showed Mozambican taxi driver, Mido Macia, being dragged on his back behind a police van. Two hours later he was found dead in his Davyton police cell. Echoes of Richard Attenborough's film CRY FREEDOM rang loud and clear. This East Rand unit serving about 150,000 people, is renowned for quick response times and for the occasional case ending in death before the culprit had been charged. Such was the case for Benoni Taxi Association member Mido Macia. According to a retired Davyton officer of 15 years senior service, *"most assaults by police were not reported."* A local motorist said, *"Davyton police officers will slap and kick you seemingly just for the fun of it, especially at night."* In his cartoon Zapiro etched the words 'S.A.'S REPUTATION' on Macia's body. Phuti Setati, the Acting Head of Communications at Davyton said, *"We acknowledge that we do have some rotten apples, but the majority of the police officers are there for the people and they are there to serve."* A nice statement, but for the fact that there are an awful lot of barrels being spoiled by rotten apples. Nine of his rotten apples were denied bail by the Benoni Magistrates Court. Bail would have released them back into the society of fellow officers who are witness to what happened. Their safety on bail is not something the State could guarantee. What an indictment of members of the police service who have taken an oath to uphold the law. The people are not happy with the police. There are some rare exceptions such as the impeccable unit under the command of Lt. Colonel Jim Wilkins at Himeville serving that village and the Underberg communities. Nationally, civil claims against the police have risen almost 70% in the last two years to a total of 5,090 cases. The South African Human Rights Commission is monitoring the situation. An extremely high-class police commander appears necessary to restore public confidence, law and order, police morale, discipline and South Africa's worldwide image.

The Independent Police Investigative Directorate (IPID) revealed in March 2013 that 'about' 932 people died in police custody in 2011-12. KwaZulu-Natal had the highest number of deaths in police custody, with 268 inmates reportedly dead in cells. There were 217 such reports from Gauteng and 120 from Eastern Cape. IPID is also investigating the death of a policeman who died in police custody at Barklay East in January, a day after he was detained for allegedly being drunk. S.A.'s reputation is in many barrels.

Police could not do anything about the principal European revolution of the 1980s and may well have been told in view of the enormity of the crowds to keep a low profile. The Berlin Wall prevented 3.5m East Germans from circumventing Eastern Block emigration laws. East Germans took a heavy hammer to the Berlin Wall and section by section it crumbled, to the delight of East and West Germans who cheered every hammer-blow, many from on top. Between its commencement in 1961 to prevent massive emigration and defection that marked Germany and the Eastern Block post-World War II, and its destruction in 1989, some 5,000 people attempted to escape East Berlin over the wall. An estimated 600 died in the effort. *"We are talking about the most important moment in the history of the late 20th century. These were days that quite literally changed the world. Berlin always was at the epicentre, not just of divided Germany nor of Europe but of the schism between East and West. It was always, in the post-war era, the frontline city of the Cold War and as such it was very likely that had there been conflict between the Soviet Union and NATO this would, in one form or another have been connected with Berlin. So, it was quite something to have been present at the moment and the place where the collapse of the Communist empire – an evil empire as far as I am concerned – really began."* Thus wrote retired Irish Guards Major General Sir Robert Corbett, KCVO, CB, and British Commandant in Berlin at the time. With a revolutionary shift in political and economic policy, German reunification was formally concluded on 3rd October 1990.

Following the 2016 election ending the Obama era in America, we witness the Trump revolution. He came to power on the ticket of making life better for the American people. The hotelier-businessman has different ideas to any predecessor and is already described as The Disruptive President. The signing of Executive Orders to build a wall between the States and Mexico, and to eject eleven million illegal immigrants from America are as good a social revolution foundation as any.

The vote by the British people to opt out of the European Union was a surprise which brought about the resignation of British Premier, David Cameron. He went for 50% + majority when he should have gone for 2/3, the amount necessary to call a General Election. The price was early retirement from Downing Street. Teresa May picked up the tab. After this revolution Britain could be much changed.

CHAPTER V

THE PEOPLE

Ethnic Origins

In order to better understand the sort of people that we are dealing with it is useful to know a little of the origins of man and the manner in which races evolved domestically, socially and geographically. Anthropologists are continually making new discoveries that date or shape the matter and which sometimes blow earlier theories 'out of the water'. In a much earlier time than we are concerned with now we have recently come to learn that cave dwellers of the South-East Coast of Africa made their way north and generation by generation explored a bit further, crossing the South of Saudi Arabia and making their way across India and Indonesia to Australia. Caucasian man of the Northern Hemisphere was not confined by a sea shore until he came to one, and that took him a long time. Water washed through the Irish Sea long before the land between France and England became soggy. Atlantic rollers eat away the soft texture of the Channel to join up with the North Sea. Baltic salmon are Atlantic salmon because the seaway between Scotland and Scandinavia had opened up millions of years earlier.

The focus of this is the people of sub-Saharan Africa and how they became the people of South Africa. The story of the Bantu tribes who swarmed in their hundreds down and across the African continent is an interesting one but the real history of it has been irretrievably lost as very few writers deemed it worthwhile during their exploration of the new continent by colonists. The Zulus would not be the people they are today but for the late emergence of a powerful Chieftain called Shaka who was invited by the Great White Queen to visit her in England and on the Isle of Wight in 1882. Inside a Caucasian suit stood a large Nguni Bantu king.

As far as Zululand was concerned, in the Victorian era a number of great Chiefs came to the fore, Shaka (d. 1828), Dingane (d. 1840), Mpande (d. 1856) and Cetswayo (d. 1884). Shaka was the illegitimate son of Senzagakona, Chief of the Zulus. He was succeeded by his half-brother, Dingane, who executed all his royal kin except Mpande, another half-brother who posed no threat.

Bitter or pleasant experience, better education, or a desire to learn from the recent white settler has imbued many natives with strong will-power to achieve something by hard work. For each that will give it a go there are many to whom work beyond the family kraal is not for them. The descendants of those who were settled in Cape Colony a little over two centuries ago appreciate today an enjoyable lifestyle and wealth that they have worked hard for. Whilst many natives have witnessed the labours of their masters, few have done any imitation. The Le Roux, Du Toit, Malherbe, Fourie families of Huguenot origin were singled out by the Dutch with whom they had gone to live after the Revocation of the Edict of Nantes. They were singled out by their hosts for those crafts and brought to Cape Colony to exercise their crafts. Huguenots have had a greater influence upon the development of wherever they settled, or were settled, than any other ethnic grouping that has ever been formed out of adversity in the field of religion, work ethic or achievement in battle. The van de Merwe, Westerhuizen and many Willems should be proud of their human resource, the ability to put a square peg in a square hole and capitalise upon it to having been the wheelwrights of the wagons that made the Great trek and the guns wheeled about in the South African wars.

South Africa is in its infancy as a developing nation. Dr A.T. Bryant in THE ZULU PEOPLE clearly gives the impression that the race as we know it today is less than two centuries old. The Zulu people were evolving from other Nguni tribes from about the time of the Battle of Waterloo, 1815. The history of their evolution was kept verbally in the absence of any means of physical written record. They did not have ink and paper. There is a great gap between the rock art drawings in caves of the San people and anything being committed to writing two thousand years later. One member of the antelope family spans that time warp. There are many rock art depictions of Eland. We see them live in the bergs with a pleasant degree of frequency today. They measure a great time-span.

Doctor Bryant writes in THE ZULU PEOPLE "that the Negro race is differentiated from the Caucasic by certain physical characteristics" and what he writes applies to Bantus, Nguni and Zulu. Coiled or spiral hair is one of the most defining items, followed by limb bones, the lower ones being longer than the upper than is the case with Europeans; the two frontal eminences of the forehead are fused and a bony elevation in the palate is present. The young Zulu is sleek and robust in build.

Sir Harry Johnston said, "The Zulu is perhaps the most typical Bantu and 'comliest' development of the true Negro."

Another anthropologist named Barrow said, "*The men are the finest figures I ever beheld…they were tall, robust and muscular; their habits of life had induced a firmness of carriage, and an open, manly demeanour, which added to the good nature that overspread their features, showed them at once to be equally unconscious of fear, suspicion and treachery. A young man about 20, of 6ft. 10in (2.083m.) was one of the finest figures that perhaps was ever created. He was a perfect Hercules; and a cast from his body would not have disgraced the pedestal of that deity in the Farnese palace.*"

Isaacs said, "*The Zoola men are, without exception, the finest race of people which Southern or Eastern Africa can furnish, or that I have ever seen. They are tall, athletic, well- proportioned and good-featured…capable of enduring great fatigue, both in war and in hunting excursions and their agility is almost beyond comprehension.*"

This attractive form has been acquired through the natural, manly life that they have led in pastoral surroundings for many generations whilst gradually moving south-east from central Africa. They have always had adequate nourishing food in a nice temperate climate. 'Athletic' is a European perception that the Zulu fails to live up to in field competition though not on the track. Few surpass the Bantu of East Africa in distance running or walking over broken country. It is possible that being strapped to the mother's back and facing forward that the child misses out on being able to change optical focus as fast as the European. Blue-eyed babies soon become brown-eyed. Charles Darwin accepted the inferiority of European eyesight. The Fuegians of deep South America had the most extraordinary power of eyesight and the African Bantu beat the American Indian. Research displayed by Professor R.S. Woodworth at the St. Louis Exposition, 1904 also revealed Zulu vision to be considerably stronger than that of Europeans, particularly in their ability to see with greater clarity at long distance. Zulu boys and girls quickly discern and detect small objects lost in dense, tall grass. It seems as though this acuity of vision is dependent upon the power of interpreting signs which are meaningless to Europeans and thus escape their observation.

Modern football is not only tainted by corruption and match-fixing but by the fact that, with few exceptions, the Bantu footballer is not as adept at the game as the European. The Zulu is a better stick fighter (as President Zuma professes), and with good training may make a good wrestler, boxer, tosser of the caber, weight or discus thrower. One interesting observation of the naturalists and anthropologists of late C.18th was that face muscles are more rigid than those of Europeans, preventing them from as great an expression of emotions. Movement of the ears and scalp is largely absent. Nothing defines the Zulu woman as significantly as the protrusion of her buttocks, considered by the male as an essential to female beauty. Katlego Sibeko in the soapbox series *Isidingo* is a prime example. The Zulu man defines the woman's buttocks as *Shikilile* (massively bulky), *iMpentsula* (far projecting), *isiBélu* (turned up due to a fine spinal curve), and *iNtsheshelezi* (none-at-all).

When born, Zulu babies are normally not 'black' (a hue of chocolate), but a pinky-yellow, the colour gradually and perceptibly darkening within the first few weeks after exposure to sunlight. Colour is almost certainly developed on account of climatic conditions. White men and white animals are consistently found inhabiting the colder regions of the world, and dark men and dark animals the hotter regions. Negroes passing from Africa to America and Europe lose their 'blackness'; Europeans (of the Indian Civil Service for example), long resident in India, acquire, even under their clothing, a touch of 'tar brush'. A few Englishmen known to the author bear this Indian touch. Skin pigmentation has long puzzled the researcher, dampness and dry atmosphere having been supposed to be the effective cause. Dr Bryant points out that 'whites' were confined to the northern and temperate lands, the 'blacks' to tropical climes. In the Northern and temperate Hemisphere there is 1½ times as much water as dry land whereas in the Southern Hemisphere there is six times as much ocean water (with a higher temperature). The great pyramid of Giza is coincidentally sited on the world's longest terrestrial land mass. How did they know? Negro man has perfected the pigmentation process through the ages in the combination of sunlight and humidity. The Caucasic European lost the power to adapt, or never had it. If 'chocolate' dark was the original colour of man, and that seems to have been fixed æons ago, then it is possible that the European became 'bleached' in the Ice Age.

The Bantu has a phenomenal sense of hearing. The old hunting Bushman got an inkling of the arrival of game that was out of sight on the other side of a steep bank. They easily identify the source of noise and categorise it accurately between feathered game, antelope species, the cat family and other humans. Their ability to smell things like the smoke from a train in the old days over several miles is acute yet they are oblivious of domestic odours that they were brought up with. These include putrid hides, rancid milk (*amasi*), and the body odour of those they live with being utterly imperceptible to their olfactory nerves. Every foreign traveller to Africa quickly becomes acquainted with the peculiar rancid scent by which the African Negro may be detected and the smoke from the rondavel fire that clings to clothing. The body odour of the brown American tribes is quite different and it is not surprising that the Bantu does not like the white man's smell. Good trackers in the Malaysian jungle during the Burma campaign of WW2 could tell which village some smells came from.

Just as the Irish believe in leprechauns, the Zulu has a few spirits which need to be kept in check. A brick wrapped in paper and placed under each bed leg prevents the naughty tokoloshe from invading the person. The tokoloshe can have an influence on a household and exorcism is occasionally necessary. The author recently experienced the gearshift in his car coming loose, trouble with the AGA stove and a 260-year-old long case clock stopping and refusing to go again despite many adjustments to its level. Made by John Bunting, of Long Buckby, Northamptonshire mid-C.18th, the clock keeps perfect time, chiming in unison with 'Big Ben' being struck on a Jacqui Lawson piece of software and the jingles announcing the news on television. The cause of the clock stopping and refusing to go again was not apparent and no amount of changing slivers of wood to ensure the mechanism was level made any difference. Some other power was at large.

A Polish friend living in Normandy half a century ago occasionally referred to someone or something 'needing a good swift kick.' It seemed inappropriate to kick the 1.6m beautifully crafted and polished English oak case that supports the clock, so the author, inspired by outer forces, struck the case a smart blow with his hand. The mechanism jumped ¼" from its secure position, taking with it on the original gut both ten pound wrought iron weights, and resettled askew. When put back in the position that Mr Bunting intended the clock to sit perfectly in and run smoothly forever, the pendulum then being activated, the clock has run accurately ever since. What, other than a tokoloshe, could have been blasted from the clock by the firm slap?

'Environment', better food and living is known to promote energy and development, including that of the brain. Athletes are encouraged towards pastas and more recently it is revealed that a shot of Ricin improves Matric results. The average cranial capacity of the C.19th Bantu race was given by researchers Quarrefages and Hany as 1,422cc, 71cc less than the negroes of the Sudan and right across to Guinea. There was only a 2cc difference between the latter and the European at 1,497cc. The French anthropologist, Topinard, found the Negro brain to weigh an average of 1,263 grams, against Keith's finding the European brain to weigh 1,480g. This 14.7% difference said little more due to the paucity of precision and discrimination. It would be erroneous to assume that cubic capacity and weight of matter were the determining factors of intelligence. Take two laptops or iPods of different manufacture, weigh them, measure them, then tell which has the most powerful processing capacity.

Sergeant Eugene McGillycuddy, Royal Munster Fusiliers, was taking his freshly brewed early morning tea near Belmont, on N 12, south-west of Kimberley in 1900. In the early morning light he was thinking to himself about the steam coming off his tea when a Boer bullet scalped him, rendering him unconscious for several days. When he came round in the military hospital his first words in his native Kerry brogue were, *"Me tay's steamin."* Now tell me how a computer knows which was the last job it was doing!

Since Phoenician times the African Negro encountered the Saudi Arabian maritime merchant and much later the Portuguese explorer, the Dutch colonialist and the English invader. Some stark differences segregate the African peoples from those who were motivated by creativity and anticipation of consequences. Those who came to Africa brought the wheel, the use of water for power and the generation of electricity [Eskom probably wish that they had brought a lot more!]. The native Bantu–Nguni has been slow to make use of these imports and the country remains excessively reliant upon what it can dig out of the ground (resources) and sell, making little use of them itself. Over 500 years after the Portuguese found that the natives lived in round houses with thatched roofs, many natives are still using this design, only substituting concrete blocks for wattle, mud and dung. By contrast, the sociological system of these peoples has shown a degree of discipline, dedication to what mattered to pastoral and military man, and duty to family and unit that would well benefit some of mankind today. Mxolisi Nene, a 20-year-old taxi driver, sneaked away his grandfather's Toyota Jazz with three friends and found himself pulling them out of the car when they were washed off the Woodhouse Road bridge into the Duzi river at 10pm. **The cause was not that the river was in flood, but ill-discipline that would not have occurred in earlier generations.** History tells us where we have been and much about our potential to go a lot further.

The native man such as our gardener, Mduduzi Mzolo, displays no lack of will to work and is a punctilious time-keeper. He has been quick to learn a wide variety of garden, horticultural and handyman skills. He is motivated by being provided with a small cottage with electricity and running water, and a living wage somewhat above the minimum guideline. When he came to us on the farm as a general agricultural labourer, he was assigned a mud-walled rondavel with a thatch roof and external ablution and washing facilities. When we sold the farm and moved on the change was a significant upgrade to a rectangular 25m^2 cottage with running water, WC, shower, electricity, cooker and garden.

I gain the feeling that a number of agricultural employers prefer the stick to the carrot, a feature emphasised by Stephen Saad, founder of Aspen pharmaceutical, in another chapter. I think that motivation may also have been at the heart of issues leading to Marikana, as evidenced at the Commission of Inquiry. Suicides amongst police officers [2010: 97; 2011: 85; 2012: 116] are a national tragedy given that the National Police Commissioner claimed before Judge Farlam that the police had a number of psychologists and other professionals on hand to attend to officers in debriefings following confrontation with criminals. The Police Minister, Nathi Mthethwa, identified that 10,636 officers suffered from depression and 2,763 suffered from post-traumatic stress disorder. The job of a South African 'bobby' is undoubtedly not a happy one. I just wonder how it compares with that of a rock-face driller on a quarter of a policeman's salary.

"What the native really suffers" said Dr Bryant in THE ZULU PEOPLE, *"is a total lack of creative and initiating mental ability."* Simple explanation; moderate nutrition and pastoral learning without exercise of the ability to read or write is not conducive to inspirational or creative thinking by a people who were stuck in the 'Western' Stone and Iron ages until they came to learn new things from the various settlers who have landed on their shores, mostly in the last two centuries. The Stone Age was when early man used a stone as a tool. Commencing about 3.4 million years ago, it ended for some as late as 2,000 B.C.

Although North Africa was influenced to certain extent by European Bronze Age cultures (for examples, traces of the Bell beaker tradition are found in Morocco), Africa did not develop its own metallurgy until the Phoenician colonization (ca. 1100 BCE) of North Africa and remained attached to the Neolithic way of life. This is often regarded as the second age of man. The civilization of Ancient Egypt, whose influence did not cover the rest of Africa, was rather an exception from this rule as regarding the whole range of ancient cultures of Africa.

In Sub-Saharan Africa, inhabitants at Termit, in eastern Niger, became the first iron smelting people in West Africa around 1500 BCE. Iron and copper working then continued to spread southward through the continent, reaching the Cape around CE 200. The widespread use of iron revolutionised the Bantu-speaking farming communities who adopted it, driving out and absorbing the rock tool using hunter-gatherer societies they encountered as they expanded to farm wider areas of savannah. The technologically superior Bantu-speakers spread across southern Africa and became wealthy and powerful, producing iron for tools and weapons in large, industrial quantities.

The *Iron Age* is the third principal period of the three-age system created by Christian Thomsen (1788-1865) for classifying ancient societies and prehistoric stages of progress. In Central Africa, iron working may have been practised as early as the 3rd millennium BCE. It was once believed that iron and copper working in Sub-Saharan Africa spread in conjunction with the Bantu expansion, from the Cameroon region to the African Great Lakes in the 3rd century BC, reaching the Cape around AD 400.

"Never blame anyone for not knowing what they have never had the opportunity of learning" is a maxim the author learned from a not-remembered source long ago. Prior to the arrival of various settlers, pastoral life was so conducted that there was no incentive to move on save to wipe out other tribes in a state of continual early warfare. Where natives are taught crafts they begin to express themselves with considerable artistic merit, one such development being that of Fay Berning at Ardmore Studios near Nottingham Road. Pottery, beadwork and painting are specialties. Pottery presently in the British Museum and made up to 9,000 years ago, is in shape and technique almost identical to that produced in Zululand just a century ago. Maybe the earlier pottery was due to Arab or Egyptian influence along the East Coast of Africa over several millennia? What the Bantu-Nguni-Zulu descendant lacked in ornamentation, they made up for in simple perfect shaping and, according to Bryant, were *"not excelled."* Basket work is no less admirable in the hands of many workers and there is a fresh move to encourage bead-work co-operatives.

A typical fire on the floor of a rondavel is formed within three large stones. Iron was found when one type of stone melted and the residue was retrieved from the ashes whilst hot. It was found to be malleable and could be worked into shapes by pounding with stones. The hotter the molten substance, the more easily it was shaped. Thus the transformation from the Stone Age to the Iron Age occurred at different times throughout the world and the forging of ferrous metal began. One who specialises in making horse shoes is known as a farrier; one specialising in other wrought ironwork is a blacksmith. The smith could cut and shape cogged wheels, a craft that led to clock making. The clock, such as the one on top of Elizabeth Tower, Palace of Westminster, whose mechanism strikes a 13½ ton bell nicknamed *'Big Ben'*, became a communal focal point wherever installed. The only larger bell in London is *Great Paul*. Big Ben was cast in Whitechapel Bell Foundry in 1858, Great Paul in 1881.

The Iron Age is the oldest of all metal workings. Iron beads were found in a pre-dynastic grave at El Gerzeh dating to about 4,700 BC. The early Bantu of North-Eastern Africa, now Zimbabwe, probably knew something of working iron before 900 AD. The method was employed by the Arabs 1,000 years earlier and the Mashonaland (Zimbabwean) Kalangas learned smelting from them and passed the craft on. *umTónga* (Smith) was as important a fellow in C.16th Bantu society as he had been to the Romans when they advanced gradually across Gaul (France) towards Britain in 55 BC bringing the trades, skills and cultures that formed Great Britain.

For the war-faring Zulus, the smith made the assegai blade by beating the metal with a stone and the assegai-maker (*iNyanga*) made the weapon by burning a hole with a hot iron rod into the shaft of various soft but strong woods (Brachylæna, Gawia, Halleria, Cyclostemon and iZizimezane. The shafts varied in length: 2½ft. (0.762m) was for close combat stabbing; 3½ft. (1.07m) was for throwing.

Before the licentious aggression of Shaka and before the appearance of 'white man', the indigenous native had a *joie de vivre* resembling utopian actual being. No living to earn, no fortune to make, no dignitaries to aspire to, no ambitions, no disappointments, no money, no Bonds, shops, taxes, police, tolls, traffic cops.

The tribesman built his own house on a site agreed with the headman of his local kraal. The women worked the field, fetched water and firewood. They lived in a law-free land devoid of lawlessness. No child went to school because there was not one. Home was school. Moral responsibilities were governed by one's own learning and that of one's neighbour's sense of honour, right and decency.

The arrival of the white man ruined the lot of the indigenous native. Robert Mugabe has a programme of 'Indigenisation' in Zimbabwe. This is written on that country's 2013 General Election day and a commentator on SKY tells the world that the indigenous native is getting restless because life is not living up to their expectations. White man told the Zulu that he was a savage and a slave. From Central and West Africa slaves were taken by the thousand to work in the sugar plantations of the West Indies and the cotton fields of the Southern States of North America. A century and a half later an unmistakable African voice answers my call to

Regimental Headquarters Irish Guards at Wellington Barracks, London. 'Gloria' came over from Sierra Leone about 26 years ago and worked for Ealing Council – then the Liberian Embassy – then the Green Jackets at Davies Street – then the MOD at Main Building – then G4 in Horse Guards and finally started working in RHQ four years ago! She retires in two years' time, so I suspect that this will be the last job. 'Gloria' is one hundred times better equipped to be appointed a Major General than Riah Phiyega, the National Police Commissioner appointed by President Zuma, ever will be.

Inside the back cover of Colonel Maxse's book SEYMOUR VANDELEUR (Heinemann, London, 1906) there are two maps of the African continent. The first of 1884 shows Sierra Leone (Place of the Lions) as being one of the first countries established as a British Possession. Fortunately for many of its people the slave trade which the Portuguese had commenced in the Congo and in Angola in 1481, was prohibited at the West Africa Conference in January the following year. Clarkson, Wilberforce and Dillwyn had formed a 'Society for the Suppression of the slave trade'. Britain and the United States had agreed to abolish the slave trade 23 years earlier. It took more than two decades for many other countries to comply. In four centuries, nine million slaves were taken from four million square miles of Equatorial Africa. Many were bred for sale to European Christian nations and many prisoners of war became slaves. Sir Bartle Frere, the British High Commissioner who issued the Zulus with the December 1878 Ultimatum that led to Isandlwana, Rorke's Drift and Ulundi, then the destruction of the Zulu army, had been to Zanzibar. His mission was to successfully suppress the slave trade there in 1872-3. It was another 17 years before the Sultan of Zanzibar decreed against slavery. Put timeously, the slave trade was still going on during the early part of the lives of the grandparents of readers born in the 1940s.

CHAPTER VI

BREAKOUT FROM CAPE COLONY

In May 1837, a month before Queen Victoria came to the Throne, it was rumoured in the Natal Settlement that Dingane was about to attack the Quadi and Phisi tribes who had fled for protection in Natal. Fortifications to protect them were established on Point St. Michael and of course Dingane sent two messengers to ascertain what it was all about. The messengers were sent back with word that the measures were purely defensive. This resulted in Dingane solemnly swearing that he never harboured the slightest intention of attacking or destroying the settlement and that he would never kill a white man.

Gardiner returned to Natal after a 19-month absence travelling and visiting England to report that King William IV (1830-37) disdained all right of sovereignty in Natal. Gardiner held a meeting at Port Natal to explain his leadership position to the settlers. Biggar, Cane and Ogle put in writing their protest at him having jurisdiction over them as Port Natal was not part of the British Dominion but a free settlement that was originally granted by Shaka and confirmed later by Dingane. Some allege that the original grant was for 'right of hunting' only.

Gardiner withdrew from Port Natal to the mouth of the Thongati River and erected a further mission station which was called Hambanathi (go with us). Towards the end of October the Secretary of State pointed out that the settlers had become subjects of Queen Victoria (1837-1901) and that it was 'extravagant' to pretend that the settlement was a free and independent state. A Doctor Smith brought a Dutch Boer called William Berg with him to Natal from the Cape and when they returned both eulogised about the rich country that they had passed through and how certain they were that the Boers of Cape colony would rush to occupy it. Piet Uys, of Uitenhage, accepted their word and subsequently instigated the emigration of the first Boers to Natal. William Berg is thus recognised as the first Boer to have visited Natal. One Boer, Vanvega, returned to Somerset after a few months' elephant shooting and told his friends about the marvellous country that they had seen. It seemed better farm land than some of the mountainous tracts of the Cape. Coincidental to this was the Emancipation of slavery by the British. The trade which began in October 1562 and saw 100,000 negroes transported in 1786, was banned by Westminster in 1807. It was banned in the colonies in 1834 and the Dutch did not like that because they harboured slaves. Hans Lange escaped across the Cape border late in the year and located himself at the junction of the Kloof Plaats, Klaas and Swart Vlei Rivers. Colonel A.B. Armstrong and a troop of the Cape Corps brought back the slaves without the use of force due to Colonel Armstrong's long experience and influence upon the Boers of the Cape frontier.

Rumours of a prospective Kaffir invasion of the Cape further unsettled the Boers and the first Voortrekkers set off east led by Piet Retief, with Uys, Maritz and Langa (Field Commondants) in charge.

They arrived in Zulu country through the Drakensberg mountains and soon opened up communication with Dingane. Their arrival changed the character of Natal from a Port Settlement to a colony and increased its importance in the eyes of the far-off British government.

Retief tried to persuade Civil Servant Francis Fynn to leave his job and accompany them. His knowledge of the various tribes that could threaten the trekkers' migration to the land of King Dingane would be most helpful. Fynn's personal desire was to return eventually to occupy his farm on the Isispingo where he would have the eventual protection of the Boers from any attack by the Zulus. His influence would have been sufficient to increase the native force of Natal and, with the Boers, defy Dingane and the Zulu nation. Retief never did his homework on Dingane. He supposed that a plain and honest representation of the Boer's case would meet with corresponding honest dealing from Dingane. He knew little of the King's wily character and even less of the continuity of Shaka's policy of keeping conquered country depopulated. Thus to ask Dingane to cede Natal to the Boers for their occupation was a request of gross naivety which greatly alarmed Dingane. The wily, cunning, devious, deceitful and disingenuous despot consented to grant the country to the Boers on condition that they would attach and recover cattle which had recently been stolen by a roving chief named Sigonyela.

Dingane attached to Retief's force some of his own followers for the purpose of observing how the Boers fought and how it might be possible to defeat them. Retief enticed Sigonyela into the 'garden' of a Mr Allison, made a prisoner of him and kept him in irons until he returned the cattle. When the Voortrekkers completed their journey to Port Natal, Retief told the settlers, *"Might is right. You few Englishmen here must submit to us the more powerful."*

CHAPTER VII

THE BATTLES

Isandlwana – Rorke's Drift – Ulundi

The ultimatum

A dispute giving rise to an ultimatum over land and social conduct led to the Zulus seizing their chance when Lord Chelmsford left his camp below the koppie of Isandlwana dangerously exposed as he went off in search of the next laager. The ultimatum had been brought about due to the antics of the adulterous wives of Chief Sihayo ka Xongo and a demand that the Zulu King would disband his army within 30 days. On 11th December 1878, the hour-long ultimatum was read to representatives of King Cetshwayo who were expected to commit it to memory. As there was no way that the Zulus could comply with the terms which expired on 11th January 1879, plans were already drawn up for the invasion of Zululand.

Colonel Pearson and his No. 1 Column forded the Thukela River that day and were attacked by a large Zulu impi which failed to synchronise their "horns of the buffalo" properly and they were driven off with heavy losses. Faring better, Colonel Evelyn Wood, V.C. moved South from his camp at Bhemba's Kop on the Blood River and met Lord Chelmsford as he rode north from Rorke's Drift. After an interview with Chelmsford, Wood returned to his base and by 20th January had moved to Thinta's Kop on the White Mfolozi River. He heard the shelling of Isandlwana by Chelmsford on his return after the battle and duly received Captain Alan Gardner's message of the loss of Isandlwana. He was to subsequently stay on Nqaba ka Hawane mountain for months. The Zulus call it *Khambula*.

Isandlwana, 22nd January, 1879.

Isandlwana followed; no British force had ever been so soundly thrashed by natives in their own country. The Zulus pounced when 24th regiment was weakened by Lord Chelmsford (formerly Sir Frederick Thesiger) going off to look for them, and his next laager, in the wrong direction. The Zulu army was commanded by King Cetschwayo's brother, Dabulamanzi. They were hidden in dead ground not far distant from the laager until found by a patrol which fired on them [For the most detailed account, see ISANDLWANA, by Adrian Greaves [ISBN 1-86842-117-1]. Old Etonian, and official war artist Lt. William Whitelock-Lloyd visited the desolate battlefield and committed to watercolour everything that he found. The pictures were added to his portfolio of the South African campaign and returned with him to the family home in Castletownsend, West Cork, Ireland.

They came to light just over a century later in Scotland when the late Judith Becher was clearing out a cupboard in her later father-in-law's house following the death of Brigadier Freddie Becher. He had been given the pictures by the artist's daughter. The Bechers were advised that the paintings were obviously of South Africa and a number of photocopies were sent to Zulu war historian, David Rattray. Judith and Richard Becher met him when he next visited London and they decided to put a most unusual book together. It was Rattray's last book before he was killed at his home, Fugitive's Drift, in January 2007. Acquisition of A SOLDIER-ARTIST IN ZULULAND, by David Rattray [ISBN 978-0-37707-2], is one of the shrewdest literary purchases the reader could make. The reason for the battlefield being one of the premier sites for historians and military observers is that it is totally unchanged in 134 years and all that took place can be seen on the ground. Visit Anzio (WW2, Italy) and the famous *Gullies, Preston's Farm, Carroceto* and *The Flyover* fought over by the Irish Guards in February 1943 are now on the verge of an industrial estate.

The brief story of Isandlwana is that Lord Chelmsford pulled out of the laager with half the force in the early morning to reconnoitre ahead for the next larger and scout for the Zulu Army. A considerable time after his departure local scouts went over a rise into 'dead' ground and found thousands of Zulus quietly hiding. The patrol fired a few ineffective shots and returned quickly the 2km to their larger to report their finding. Almost before the camp soldiers and artillery were in position the Zulu impis advanced across the open ground with horns spreading left and right to cut off any retreat. Sheer weight of numbers overran the camp and the right horn forced the few soldiers that could flee over the Buffalo River. Lieutenants Melvill and Coghill were ordered by Colonel Pulleine to get the Queen's Colour to safety. The colour was lost until recovered a fortnight later. Both officers were awarded posthumous V.C.s 28 years later.

In the aftermath much change was brought about in the British camp and although heavily outnumbered, they began winning victories. Little was known in London about what was going on in South Africa. It took at least 10 weeks for a message to travel to London and back. When *Illustrated London News* eventually published the war artist's impressions, the nation was horrified.

Snatching up one of the bloody assegais, a warrior would dash on to a fresh encounter. Such was the fate of most of the 1,774 men committed on the British side to the battle. No less than 1,329 perished on the field or thereabouts; 52 British officers lost their lives and as few as 55 white men managed to escape. Isandlwana was not so much a British blunder but a great Zulu victory. Not one private soldier in the 24th's firing line lived to tell the tale. Seldom in the annals of history has there been a more ghastly scene of carnage. It is probable that over 2,000 Zulus were killed. Cetshwayo's beloved regiments were 'cut-up' somewhat and in their finest hour the Zulu army spent itself for ever.

They had captured all the British supplies plus some 800 Martini-Henry rifles and half a million rounds of ammunition, little realising what resources they had captured could well have further devastated England's military ambition in Zululand.

Rorke's Drift

That dark, moonless night some 4,000 Zulus relentlessly attacked the Mission Station of Rorke's Drift which also contained stragglers from Isandlwana. Two officers, Lieutenants Chard, R.E. and Gonville

Bromhead, and about a hundred men held Rorke's Drift all night, saving the lives of the 35 sick in the missionary hospital by breaking down internal walls to free them from the fire in the thatched roof. After the Zulu withdrawal at first light of the next day, the British army took stock of the situation and eleven Victoria Crosses were awarded (seven to men of the 24th), a record for a single action. Seventeen men died on the British side. Hundreds of Zulus were killed, 351 being buried the following afternoon. Educated and enlightened Zulus of today know what happened 134 years ago. Had they thought about it the Zulus could have overrun the post at Helpmakaar and destroyed the rest of the British force. Had they known where Thesiger's force was on its way back to Isandlwana, they could have ambushed and destroyed it. By the time the British were able to return to the battlefield site six months later, accompanied by war artist Lieutenant William Whitelock-Lloyd, there were hundreds of picked human skeletons that are now buried in graves marked only by piles of white-painted stones. A splendid memorial to the Zulus is sited on the lower slope of the koppie.

On the way back to camp the Zulus who had killed one or more of the enemy made themselves apparent by doffing their skin girdles (*umuTsha*) and penis covers (*umNeedo*) and carrying them with their assegai with which they had done the deed, blade uppermost. Their Captains called upon them to rid themselves of all evil consequences by dipping their fingers in a concoction of certain medicinal herbs, lick them and spit out in the direction of the sun. Now 'clean', they replaced their girdles and penis covers and were sufficiently safe to venture into the King's presence. One should take note that this was happening in the time of our great-grandfathers and not more than a generation earlier. When Dr Bryant was researching THE ZULU PEOPLE, men who had been at Isandlwana in their 20s were now in their 70s to 80s, but there were very few of them. A generation later David Rattray interviewed some grandsons of those present at Isandlwana.

Those who had not made a killing or who had been incapacitated by the foe were 'dismissed' and sent home. Those with one or more victims to their credit marched straightway to the Grand 'Palace' of the King. They wore a sprig of wild asparagus for each victim and as many captured assegais as there were personal victims. With the warriors arrayed in the King's kraal, the army chiefs delivered a flamboyant account of their great victory, even if the force had been given a drubbing by their foe. His Majesty being frequently 'hoodwinked' or otherwise impressed, dismissed the army to go to their homes. Fighting glory had a price. Before a warrior could re-enter his home he had to somehow secure sexual intercourse with someone (old women and herd boys being easy prey) to wipe himself clean of the abdominal ailment which would otherwise result from his actions on the battlefield. Until he has accomplished intercourse he has to wander about the veld and sleep rough. Even when at last fit to enter his home still wearing his asparagus sprig and holding his assegai point upwards, the family knew that he had killed and that he was not yet a fit and proper person to return into their peaceful society. The warrior took himself to the hut of any old woman and resided with her. A further course of medicines from the *Sangoma,* abstinence from *amaSi,* the milk of a cow still suckling her calf, and eating the first fruits of the season (pumpkin and gourd) and from drinking any beer brewed from fresh grain until he shall have fortified himself by taking certain medicines. He could now wear with pride the *umNyezane* necklet proclaiming him a hero, treat himself to a new girdle and show that he could feed on the meat of a white goat as well as anyone.

Ulundi

Six months after Isandlwana the British had still not subdued the Zulus. There had been no trouble between the two races until difficulties arose between the Boers and the Zulus which, if proper action was not taken King Cetshwayo might overrun Zululand at great cost to the British. On the Natal bank of the Tugela River on 11th December 1878, John Shepstone, brother and Deputy of the Secretary for Native Affairs, Sir Theophilus Shepstone (after whom Port Shepstone is named), held a meeting to give the Zulus an ultimatum that they were unlikely to accept. A Boundary Commission had found against the Boers and that put them out of contention.

Skirmishes continued and the time came to force the Zulus to fight. Many wrongly believed that they would not do so. The chief Zulu settlement of Ulundi containing the Grand Place of King Cetshwayo lay across the Mfolozi River. The settlement, the King and his army had to be subdued. After crossing the river at 6.45am, the 2nd Division of over 5,000 men including 500 of General Wood's Flying Column and 100 of Baker's Horse, plus 12 field guns and 2 Gatling* Guns marched out into the open plain and formed a rectangle with the widest part facing Ulundi. A small detachment of cavalry and infantry including Captain Tomasson was sent out to draw the Zulus on. They got back into the Square by the skin of their teeth. An hour later vanquished Zulus were in mass retreat, forsaking their homestead of Ulundi.

The 7th Baron Braye of Stanford Hall, Leicestershire, had some 40 years ago a lovely big bay horse called *Lancer,* which his daughter, the Honourable Penny Verney-Cave, used to ride at exercise. Her father had served as a Major in 13/18th Lancers in WW2. The naming of the horse is reminiscent of the fact that there were some pitfalls in the pursuit of the Zulus who retreated from the withering fire from Brigadier-General Wood's fighting square on the plain before the settlement called Ulundi. As they raced headlong towards a donga, half a Zulu regiment, posted there to cover the retreat, rose from the long grass and let forth a volley that emptied several saddles. It was fatal for the young Captain, the Honourable Edmund Verney Wyatt-Edgell who was gallantly leading his men. The sight of him falling spurred on his men more furiously to take immediate and bloody vengeance. He is remembered in the church of Stanford-on-Avon.

It is a shocking fact that most of the wounded Zulus were killed, mostly by men of the Natal Native Contingent (also mostly Zulu). British soldiers found wounded and pretending-to-be-dead Zulus in the thickets and summarily shot them. They knew what the Zulus had done to some 1,329 officers and men at Isandlwana – disembowelled them as part of the Zulu's post-combat battle ritual.

---

* Invented in 1861 by Richard Gatling, the gun is one of the best known early manual rapid-fire weapons and a forerunner of the modern machine gun. It is known for its use by the Union forces at the siege of Petersburg during the American Civil War in the mid-1860s. Mounted on a two-wheel square axle, the six to ten barrels of the gun rotated around a central cylindrical column when a cranking handle was turned. A cam system fed each cartridge from an overhead cylindrical hopper into the barrel where it was locked, cocked and fired before extraction discarded the empty cartridge case. Sir Hiram Maxim produced the first self-powered automatic firing machine gun in 1885, and by 1911 the Gatling gun was declared obsolete.

So terminated the prime conflict between Britain and the Zulus often known as the second Anglo-Zulu war, the first having been 40 years earlier against Dingane. The indigenous people and those who settled on their land came to terms with each other. The next conflict was less than 20 years off, a similar gap to that between WW1 and WW2.

CHAPTER VIII

MAJOR POLITICAL AND INDUSTRIAL CHANGES

The Boers who had established themselves in Natal in 1842 after trekking there were unhappy about the annexure of the province after only three years in 1845. They moved out to join other Boers who were settling between the Orange and Vaal Rivers. Sir Harry Smith, British Governor of Cape Colony, annexed that country to Cape Colony. The Boer Republic of Transvaal came into being from the 1852 Sand River convention. It took the Boers six years to make up their minds about a President and finally Wessels took office in 1852. Two years later the Bloemfontein Convention brought the Orange Free State into existence. Various quarrelsome Boer elements formed three break-away mini-republics of Lydenberg, Utrecht and Zoutpansberg. Boer infighting led the British to consider taking over the Transvaal.

Diamonds were discovered in 1867 in the Orange Free State and Britain declared this land theirs in defence of the rights of the native owner in 1871. In 1877 Britain followed up this measure by annexing the Transvaal, a country in a parlous state both financially and militarily, the Transvaalers having suffered defeat at the hands of the native Chief Pedi. The annexation was a grievous insult to Boer nationalism and so they rebelled. They raised their flag over Heidelberg and subsequently defeated the British at Majuba Hill, 27th February 1881. General Colley, who had rejected an armistice with Kruger and got the 92nd Highlanders, the 58th and the Blue Jackets to the top of the mountain in the dark, misjudged the information fed him by Lt. Ian Hamilton of A Coy. The Boers climbed the adjacent koppie and launched an attack which drove the Highlanders off Majuba Hill with great loss. So sure were they of supremacy over the Boers that they had failed to dig in. A Boer bullet in the centre of his head ended General Colley's career as he walked towards them carrying his revolver. The Boers had won a superb victory. The 1st Boer War dragged on a little longer without much fighting taking place and hostilities were terminated by the Pretoria Convention in August 1881, the Transvaal remaining a British Colony. Vexation within both camps remained rife and led to the 2nd Boer War commencing in 1899.

Germany commenced establishing trading posts in 1883 in Namibia which came under their protection the following year, thus arousing British suspicions as to her intentions. In 1884 Germany annexed all the territory between the Orange River and Portuguese Angola (except Walvis Bay). In response Britain annexed from Bechuanaland, now Botswana, to the Cape Colony the following year.

Around this time massive gold deposits were found below the Witwatersrand in Transvaal and a 'gold rush' commenced. The influx unsettled the Boers and along came De Beers mining group Chairman Cecil Rhodes, Prime Minister of Cape Colony. Rhodes saw a union of South Africa as in Imperial Britain's best interests. The Boers had a different agenda for the natives to that of the British. They had objected to the abolition of slavery and they wished to treat three-quarters of a million natives as practical slaves. The Boers abused the flag of truce and habitually shot down native women. The lands and cattle of native friends and foes alike were seized, sold and stolen. The Boers were in contempt of the indigenous native and not for their own good, far too many of them harbour this resentment today.

In 1893 Kruger was re-elected for a second term as President of Transvaal. The *Uitlanders* (mostly British immigrants) found in Rhodes a good leader but his desire to cause an uprising in the Transvaal faltered. Even *The Times* newspaper crossed the line between journalism and actively supporting one side. A raid by Dr Jameson was a total failure largely due to the inebriated state of the participants. Germany supported Kruger and the Boers against the British. Various political manoeuvres led to Sir Alfred Milner, British representative at the Cape, meeting with Kruger at Bloemfontein in

May 1899. Kruger was reported as having had little intention of negotiating any question regarding *Uitlanders* or Boer rights and with the British strengthening their garrison in the country to 14,500 badly paid and generally badly fed men now armed with Lee Enfield Mk II rifles and Lyddite artillery shells. By comparison with their prospective Boer adversary, they were uneducated, unhealthy, lacking in ambition and poorly trained. To a large rolling country the British government sent infantry and artillery when cavalry and dragoons would have done the job quicker. The Second Boer War rumbled on for nearly two years inclusive of the capture of the *Morning Post* correspondent, Mr Winston Churchill, at Chieveley, near Estcourt and his escape from custody in Pretoria. The relief of Ladysmith was commemorated 105 years later by the Freedom of the Emnambithi Municipality (represented by Councillor Mrs Mazibuko) being granted to the Irish Guards. Queen Victoria commanded that a regiment of Irish Guards be formed in April 1900 to commemorate the lives of "my brave Irish soldiers". The fourth regiment of foot guards was formed of many officers and men from other Irish regiments and first mounted guard in the 64th year of Queen Victoria's reign. Queen Elizabeth II has reigned for 65 years. Field Marshal the Right Honourable Earl Roberts of Kandahar and Pretoria and the City of Waterford, VC, KG, KP, PC, GCB, OM, GCSI, GCIE was appointed first Colonel of the Irish Guards on 17th October 1900. The present Colonel is H.R.H. Prince William, Duke of Cambridge, KG., a former Officer of the Royal Air Force.

CHAPTER IX

CIVIL STRIFE

Crime

South Africa has the 9th highest prison population in the world and, with 160,000 inmates, the largest on the African continent, according to correctional services minister, S'bu Ndebele. Some 48,000 (30%) of them are awaiting trial. Every month 23,000 are released and 25,000 enter gaol, a net gain of 2,000/month. Increasing numbers of women are imprisoned for killing their husbands/partners and in over 70% of murder cases the victim and assailant are known to each other. In some cases daughters are imprisoned as convicted accomplices. Abusive behaviour by husbands is the prime motivation in a land where the woman is man's beast of burden, daily fetching huge bundles of firewood and water for domestic use while the man sits at home or tends cattle.

Crime statistics for our small KwaSani rural municipal area far removed from the metropolis of Durban and Pietermaritzburg indicate it to be one of the safest in the country. People moving out to reside nearer areas of higher population will have to adjust rapidly to the changed circumstances where the effects of high unemployment force a lot of the young to devise means of accomplishing a living. The funding of illicit habits is one of life's necessities. In this rural area there is the occasional heist at one of the two banks, probably due either to collusion with a member of a local security company, or attributable to their negligence. Sometimes the principal security firm has made a robbery look a 'piece of cake'. One day I called their manager to come and watch what I considered was about to take place. Having filled a large holdall with cash for the tills at the local supermarket, the employees left the bank and dumped the holdall in the rear of a bakkie. As the security firm's manager left the bank with me, ignoring eye contact with his employees, the two guards re-entered the bank to sign out. I walked forward to the vehicle and tapped the bag twice. An embarrassed manager made amends to his employees' routine.

On another occasion the principle security firm was in receipt of a tip-off for a heist at the same bank. As the robbers left the bank a guard challenged and was shot and wounded. The robbers got into their blue VW Golf and sped off along R 617 towards Pietermaritzburg unmolested, or pursued. Bulwer police, 30km distant were alerted to expect a blue VW Golf passing through in a hurry. It never arrived. The stolen get-away vehicle was found parked in the forest 15km distant with the keys still in the ignition. It was a fairly easy way of acquiring R55,000.

There is the occasional domestic break-in, a number of domestic disputes, the occasional assault and illegal hunting parties. Some are alcohol-related, others for 'sport' pleasure and betting. The dog that pulls down a common reed buck commands a five-figure sum. When the statistics are held up against those provided by Statistics SA, they indicate that this remote area nestling in the Drakensberg foothills 25km from the border with the Kingdom of Lesotho is a relatively safe one to live in. Many more cattle are stolen than motor cars. Those parked with the keys left in the ignition rarely trigger a second glance. Shopping left in full view of passers-by in the town centre is not snatched and the personal care that was exercised a decade ago when some carried a personal firearm, has fallen by the wayside. Windows and doors can be left unlocked so long as a maid or gardener is about to see what the guard-dog is making a fuss about. Alas there comes a time when lapses in security are punished by vandalism. A chainsaw gets nicked from the rear of a bakkie or a camera disappears from the compartment of an unlocked car in the evening. Alert dogs prevent more crime than S.A.P.S. Some of them are 'handcuffed' by drug-related incidents and a case has to be opened to initiate the paperwork necessary to secure a prosecution. The Station Commander is now a 'militarised' Colonel, being supported by Captains, Warrant Officers, Sergeants and Constables. That the National Police Commissioner is automatically a General without a day's service to her name puts 'militarised' police in the wrong light in a country that two decades after the end of Apartheid, is trying to normalise under civilian lines, leaving the military to professional soldiers. Even they got a hammering (13 dead) in Bangui, C.A.R., isolated and unsupported by their own government. South Africa would like to model its police in many ways on the British Bobby. British Bobbies have been sent to South Africa to assist. This is a complete waste of the British taxpayer's money when SAPS officers are seen on TV to pick up off the road without wearing gloves such pieces of evidence as recently discharged firearms following a taxi service turf war in North Durban. The evidence is immediately compromised by the presence of the officer's fingerprint and DNA.

Some of us were brought up in the era of 'Dick Barton – Special Agent'. Others find Inspector Clouseau more refreshing. 'Dixon of Dock Green' (Jack Hawkins) captivated the British nation like no other. Another old-fashioned police part was excellently played by Inspector Fowler (Rowan Atkinson) when he detailed Constable Habib (Mina Anwar) duties that might have had consequences of an Asian tone about them which the station commander had not thought through. One thing that one does not see in South Africa is police officers patrolling the streets in pairs yet there are plenty of vehicles marked VISIBLE POLICING. Police vehicles run up a good mileage often containing five or six personnel and when they park, it is frequently outside the local supermarket for refreshments. The low-profile adopted in rural areas definitely has its merits. Close liaison with Community Watch and a few reliable informers helps generally to keep the lid on crime. A local doctor's house was broken into recently and her business laptop stolen. The police know the most likely suspect and are just waiting for him to come out of hiding. Spasmodic roadside checks by SAPS and their traffic colleagues, Road Traffic Inspectorate, yields up varying quantities of information. Some wish it happened more often, others are offended at being stopped when lawfully going about their business or leisure. There will always be 'extreme' calls. *"Cut his balls off!"* – *"Shoot his bloody dog!"* – *"Stupid white woman, crossing a double white line,"* had an unnecessary racist tone and alienated the driver somewhat. The expression was made by an officer visiting the area. The local RTI officers were not impressed by the language and probably know best how to address the matter. If the word 'white' is dropped from the statement, it will be an improvement.

At much the same time as the British Statistical Office reported a 70,000 increase in unemployment between December 2012 and February 2013 to 2.56 million, workers in the Sobantu suburb of Pietermaritzburg stoned police, burned tyres and blockaded roads demanding jobs at the new Illovo sugar factory which is not yet open for business. Workers in nearby factories could not get to their jobs and the blockade caused massive disruption to early morning traffic. Three schools in Sobantu were closed as teachers and pupils could not get to school. A spokesperson for the Education Department described the situation as 'unfortunate' – possibly the understatement of the day, seeing the needs of education. The protesters also demanded that jobs be reserved for Sobantu residents only. Protesters claimed that local employers should be giving 'promised' jobs to local people and not outsiders. An underlying aspect of the trouble is discontent with a local councillor who had received threats that her car and her home would be burned. The councillor is alleged not to work with the branch executive committee, but with her own people. When Mayor Chris Ndlela tried to calm things down he was heckled. Police used stun grenades and rubber bullets to bring the situation under control. How long before another situation gets out of control and the nation has another 'Marikana' on its hands?

Gauteng Toll Roads

In the issue of e-tolls on the Gauteng high roads, nothing has disturbed public suspicion so much as the fact that the government pushed the project through so quickly with almost no public consultation bar a few newspaper adverts in 2007. The resulting fight between the public and the government has meant that the e-tolls, which were due to have commenced operation in 2011 have had to be delayed several times. The roads agency, Sanral, is losing out on about R200m/month and has subsequently received downgrades from credit agencies. All for a matter of consultation with those affected.

This is an example of the government's desire to haul motorists into line with the needs of taxation in the nationwide implementation of Toll Roads. There are already tolls on a number of national roads and one pays according to use. At phenomenal cost the government has bought in from Germany a sophisticated system and applied it firstly to the national roads in the Gauteng province containing Pretoria and Johannesburg as the principal cities, one of government, the other of commerce, with great emphasis on mined resources.

The South African motorist is rebelling. To fund the road costs by way of a small addition to the fuel levy would cost absolutely nothing in collection fees. Collection costs amount to nearly 40% of what motorists will pay for tolling. The motorist sees the collection of fees as a scam for the enrichment of a few. Within the African continent, South Africa is by a long way the foremost country of fraud practitioners. Nigeria comes a very poor second. The collection of R5bn worth of fees goes offshore to Kapsch in Austria, owners of 83% of Electronic Toll Collection. It is far from the Auditor General's reach and oversight powers. A petrol/diesel levy would stay in South Africa and be audited. Fuel levies are the fourth biggest generator of income for the government. A 15-cent increase in highways levies would have been sufficient to pay for improvements to Gauteng's roads. If government had ring-fenced all fuel levies for the past decade, it could have done the job already. What happened to the money? It went to bail out the state airline (SAA) and to build a freeway to the President's bolt-hole village of Nkandla, already the beneficiary of over R200m of taxpayer's money. R200m is the monthly interest charge on the installation cost of the unused e-toll gates.

Exporting R5bn impoverishes the country when Current Account is already in deficit. R40bn is already collected by government in fuel levies, more than is needed to sustain decent road structures. Tolls are another disguised tax topping what has already been paid for the year.

For-profit taxis are exempt from the proposed toll that those producing the country's wealth have to pay. Government Ministers are as scared of taxes as anyone. Tax collected may not amount to that which is necessary for the government to have good parties, rounding off the evening with the best of Blue Label. The motorist feels powerless, knowing that the latest scheme is like many predecessors, no contract details being made public just as Eskom entered into a contract with BHP Billiton to buy electricity at half the cost of production until 2028.

The motorist is making a plan. Plan A – Motorists should not register for e-toll tags, as registration is not a legal requirement anyway. If one does not register, an account will be sent for passing through a toll without paying. That could be 300,000 accounts per day or 10 billion accounts in the year. No government has yet managed that. Plan B follows!

When sent an account, query it. The toll operator will have to send a photograph of every toll that the car has passed through. Do the figures and they come to 20 billion in total. On receipt of the photograph, argue that it was not you but a cloned number plate and demand proof that the said car was driven by you. Demand that LETTERS OF DEMAND be sent by Registered Post. Defend the case if you can spare the time. Insist in writing that the person in charge of the camera attends Court and be prepared to pay your R15 (£1.07 @ R14:£1) the day before the hearing. It will never reach that stage, the logistics and costs being too overwhelming. Over 20 years there is perhaps R160 billion at stake here, and many times that when every province is involved.

The consortium rebelling against the new tolls demonstrate clearly that funds for roads could be much more easily raised than the South African motorist being milked by the European consortium that got the contract of which few details are available. They are adamant that motorists cannot be locked up for not complying with the legislation and that if all motorists club together, the government cannot win. Furthermore, the more draconian the authorities, the more they will alienate motorists. The run-up to a General Election is not the time to incur bad press. The prospect of losing power is matched by the fear of losing what is most enjoyed now – the power to plunder the State. The government may have got it wrong on e-tolling. It works in limited circumstances such as on the Dublin ring road and the new M6 Expressway. Initial Toll plans collapsed in the U.K. and Spain but have been implemented in Austria, Poland, the Czech Republic and Australia. Insufficient numbers of the four million unemployed in South Africa have the ability to join a team managing all the toll gates collecting money electronically all over South Africa. It's just asking too much. At a Tolling Forum in Johannesburg at the end of April the general consensus was that tolling is a failed project. When attendees were asked to raise their hands in a pro/anti vote even Busani Ngcaweni from the Deputy President's Office half raised his hand when asked who was against the e-tolls. No hands were raised for a 'pro' vote. The most unhappy aspect of the whole saga is that the Austrian-based operator, Kapsch, will make most of the profit. Some of Kapsch's shares are held by its Swedish subsidiary, SAAB – a company accused of kickbacks in SA's notorious arms deal fiasco.

The Church has entered the political fray several times over the years. The most brilliant episode was Bishop Rubin, of Durban, sending packing a Chinese ship loaded with arms for Zimbabwe. Foreign arms may not be transported from a South African Port to another land-locked country. Someone thought that if the arms were unloaded they would have to be transported inland. Bishop Rubin was not going to have any arms unloaded in his Diocese.

More recently the Catholic Church has joined the fray of those opposed to e-tolling in Gauteng. The Justice and Peace wing of the SA Catholic Bishops' Conference called for the immediate suspension of e-tolling and a "full access review".

Transport Minister, Ben Martins, told the National Council of Provinces that e-tolling is needed to pay for and maintain infrastructure critical to the country's future economic growth. *Business Day* reported that the National Council had adopted a bill against objections by opposition parties. The economy requires infrastructure to develop and grow, create jobs and curtail unemployment and inequality. With a growing budget deficit it becomes necessary to find other means of funding expansion. The Minister said nothing about either establishment costs or the foreign element of collection of tolls. The government has stated that Sanral's creditors will be paid whether tolls are implemented or not.

It is unlikely that any shots will be fired but you can see who is calling the shots. The Transport and Related Matters Amendment Bill needs to be finalised. Then the Transport Minister can announce the tariffs. When the case presented by the Opposition to Urban Tolling Alliance (OUTA) is heard in the Supreme Court, e-tolls may be declared illegal. OUTA has spent R8.4 million of private citizens' money fighting the tolls whilst the government's case defended by David Unterhalter and Jeremy Gauntlett is funded by the taxpayer. Typical of South African government; the cart is put before the horse. The latest is that tolls for light vehicles will be reduced by 18.2%

It is difficult to know from what point one should start to take seriously such reports in the daily press. Factory output is just as captivating. In the latest recorded year, manufacturing production rose only 2.2%. This is below the 2.6% forecast by 13 economists polled by Bloomberg. 68,000 jobs were shed in Q4 with the possibility that the total could rise further. Well, it is obviously doing so. If Lonmin had retrenched 14,000 as planned, the total for that Quarter would have been 82,000. South African economist Elna Moolman (Renaissance Capital) sees the political environment as particularly restraining to growth. Moolman described manufacturing *'as one of the sectors – along with mining and agriculture, in which we may see job losses in 2013'.* The chickens are coming home to roost.

South Africa is the largest economy of the African continent but the smallest member of the BRIC countries which it recently joined. Brazil, Russia, India and China see South Africa as a 'gateway' to the rest of the continent. 2.2% growth is small for the BRIC countries. It is too small for the good of South Africa where government said that it wanted 7% to make a dent in unemployment. The Treasury can only produce figures showing a third of what is needed. Little wonder that there is talk of some current Matric achievers never achieving a permanent job in their life.

As the months go by the news does not get any better. By mid-April 2013 consumer confidence in South Africa plunged to a nine-year low during Q1. The perceived message is that household spending, the main driver of the economy, will be subdued for the rest of the year. Not even at the height of global fiscal crisis in 2008 were consumers as downbeat about the country's economic prospects and their own personal household finances as they are now, and that's the opinion of the chief economist at First National Bank, Sizwe Nxedlana. Such news is on the dark side and so long as the public are preoccupied with the Nkandla scandal, tolling in Gauteng and fracking in the Karoo, nobody is going to notice.

Anyone thinking that the author only writes of doom and gloom would not expect him to notice the things that are going well, a feature of economics mentioned previously. Foreigners are net buyers of R12.773 bn. worth of local bonds so far this year, and of R4.415bn worth of local shares. These purchases shore up the FDI necessary to closed the trade gap. It is important to remember that bonds and shares are exchangeable for cash at short notice; the trade gap is not. Some of this gap may be closed by the fact that Richard's Bay coal terminal saw a 20% year-on-year surge in tonnage shipped to 7.5 million tons in March. Transnet National Ports Authority reported bulk exports having risen in the past year to 13.8 million tons. That is the highest level achieved since October 2011. Figures like these stand between the current status quo and unemployment going to 30%.

Overseas investors could be forgiven for not understanding the language of the South African government. We learned at the Manguang party conference that in Land Reform jingo, 'Willing buyer – Willing seller' means 'Equitable Settlement'. Internationally we have come to learn that Quantitative Easing means 'Printing Money' and issuing Gilts. It can also mean the Bank of England making money available electronically to the banks. The mind boggles at the thought of receiving from BoE an e-mail stating that £5bn has been credited to your account for outward lending. Nationalisation of Mines was packed away at Manguang only to be replaced a few days later by the Mineral and Petroleum Resources Development Amendment Bill (MPRDA). In this little piece of legislation that rattles the corridors of the mining industry with uncertainty, it is stated that the amendments relate to 'increased ministerial control and bureaucracy, an export licensing regime and timetables as ineffective as 30% of white-owned farms being transferred to natives by 2014. When the government interfered with the diamond industry, cutters and polishers fell from 2,500 in 2005 to about 500 eight years later. The MPRDA Bill proposes that the Minister should follow share trading in mineral companies. It raises the question that maybe the Minister would be better employed looking after people, not public companies.

An unusual headline in the 'Money and Careers' sector of *Sunday Times* (Feb. 10) caught my eye, for I have spent more time short of money than well endowed, have had a varied career and ended owing the tax man nothing. "*SARS must wait in line*" said the report on a recent court judgement in SARA v. Beginsel NO and others. A new precedent was established in terms of which SARS must wait in line for payment with all other unsecured creditors. Graeme Palmer, Senior Associate at law firm Garlicke and Bousfield explained that, in most cases, companies accumulated tax liabilities in the ordinary course of business. There was a loophole in the law for SARS – as the regulator investigating offences – to become a preferred creditor. This was justified when the taxpayer had concealed its true state of affairs.

Business Rescue may have failed with *1time* airline despite statistics indicating that more than half of all business rescue applications ending in a happy outcome. Much like Debt Review for individuals, Business Rescue is intended to give ailing businesses some breathing space from creditors. The subtle difference is between 'ailing' and 'failure'. The focus of Business Rescue is upon saving a company and jobs, rather than satisfying creditors. Business Rescue buys a company three months. At that point, survival must be possible or the rescue practitioner must report, showing why the business should continue to operate. 75% of creditors must have agreed to the turnaround proposals in the first place. SARS is often one of the prime creditors when the company has a cash crisis. Sometimes a company tries to file for liquidation only to find that other affected parties go to Court to force the business rescue into action. The best means of a creditor getting money back is for the business rescue to be successful, and if SARS is just an ordinary creditor, it may be their best chance too.

Municipalities have been up to all sorts of tricks to 'square the hole'. Examining every ratepayer's status, they unilaterally adjust the category of the property into the highest category. By the time the ratepayer comes to examining why rates have escalated radically, the higher rate has to be paid pending an appeal process. Someone living in a rural agricultural zone growing vegetables as a hobby for supply to the local supermarket to enhance personal income is re-rated from agricultural to residential, the latter category attracting a 260% rise in rates for no additional benefit. The municipality says that the prime use of the agricultural sub-division is 'residential'. No more 'greens'!

One would have thought that everything possible would be done to encourage tourism operators to expand their business. Wrong! The municipality says that the business proprietor's home, which is also their business premises, is primarily a residential property and therefore attracts a higher rate than 'tourism and accommodation'. It does not matter to the municipality if the retired farmer doing horticulture succeeds or fails due to billowing rates costs. It does not matter to the municipality if the tourism facilitator gives visitors such a pleasant experience that they return to the district again or if their business is overwhelmed by fuel and administrative costs.

One would also have thought that, with so few passing the Auditor General's tests to a clean bill of health, their Mayors would be more selective in what to do to avoid annual audits being 'qualified'. In going through its contracts with local suppliers, KwaSani Municipality in the rural Southern Drakensberg found that a contract had been awarded for community security without going through the appropriate tender process. Despite the relationship between Principal and sub-contractor having been established several years earlier under a previous Mayor, the present regime decided last year to arbitrarily pull the rug from under the feet of the service supplier whose negotiated fee for excellent service was some R670,000.

Appropriately-named Community Watch employed two people using state-of-the-art radio equipment that linked all farmers, the police, traffic cops, security companies, local fire service and other interested parties in one 'military' network. It worked superbly especially in circumstances where a minute lost in controlling a run-away veldt fire could amount to an hour in bringing the situation under control. In the dry months of winter, daily reports of weather conditions are given out on the farmers' network in the early morning, enabling farmers to make a plan for the day. Often a breeze blows up around the middle of the day just as everyone is taking a lunch-break. Meteorological equipment at the Community Watch office gives notice of such changes and these are passed on to the farming community. In the occasional event of advice of a run-away fire, Community Watch warns downwind farmers and nearest neighbours on the network focus their attention on back-burning when necessary. In a major emergency the combined forces of Working-With-Fire and aerial reconnaissance come into play. A large Russian-made helicopter can scoop 3,000lt. of water from the nearest dam and drop it ahead of an advancing inferno within minutes.

A sub-section of Community Watch is mountain rescue orientated and thus capable of accessing inhospitable parts of the Drakensberg in the event of an aircraft going missing or a tourist lying on a rocky lintel, immobilised by a broken leg.

A Special General Meeting was called by Community Watch at Underberg Country Club and chaired by local farmer Chris Barras, a man well-versed as a Quantity Surveyor and builder in Pietermaritzburg and Durban before marrying a farmer's daughter, Norajean Campbell, some 35 years ago. The local Mayor and councillors were invited to attend. The Mayor and two Democratic Alliance Councillors put in a worthwhile appearance. When answering questions the Mayor spelled out the Municipality's side of the situation but gave little guidance upon the arbitrary withdrawal of funds seven months previously, or the Municipality's lack of communication with Community Watch, or reason for entering protracted litigation for the sole benefit of lawyers and most probably funded by the ratepayers.

The Chairman proposed that the litigation process might be suspended to enable the parties to discuss the matter rationally. The Mayor advised that such a proposal would have to have the approval of the municipal council. Nobody objected to his adherence to complying with protocol. When pressed for a time-frame by a ratepayer, the Mayor became evasive and gave the impression that the matter could be resolved sometime in the future, rather than be proactively addressed in the best interests of the ratepayers. Fundamental to the issue of Community Watch is personal freedom and security of the people of the community as enshrined in the Bill of Rights, the backbone of the Constitution of South Africa. In all probability the Mayor has the same duty of care over the citizens of his municipality as the President does over those who reside in South Africa. Section 12.1 of the Bill of Rights says, *"Everyone has the right to freedom and security of the person."* Thus, where a municipality does not take every reasonable step to ensure the freedom and security of its people, it can be said to be failing in its duty of care.

Corruption and violence are by no means unique to South Africa. It is far more scary drawing cash from an ATM in Bogotá than Pietermaritzburg. South Africa is a 'safe' country by comparison. Well, one would have thought so but for learning from the media of panga attacks at a school. Gang warfare in the Thornville area south of Pietermaritzburg. Young (16) Siyanda Sithole was saved from panga-wielding pupils by the school cook who slammed the door on his attackers. Zwelihle Mkize (17) was rescued by a teacher after he was stabbed in the back three times and also taken to hospital. It was the third such incident of the year and the school governing body Chairperson says, *"it is difficult to know what the problem is."* Gangs are as old as man's social groupings and children take pride in their sense of belonging to a gang. If pangas and knives are part of school life before morning assembly, one dreads to think what the end of the day will bring. The violence and weaponry are a serious reflection on society. It may even be considered a form of Civil War.

It was from Estcourt, a small town about halfway between Harrismith and Pietermaritzburg, that reports first came by telephone and telegram of the disaster involving an armoured train that was ambushed by the Boers near Chieveley on 15th November 1899. A nine-pounder naval gun from H.M.S. *Tartar* formed the main armament of an armoured train that was accompanied by a Company of the 2nd Bn. Dublin Fusiliers and a Company of the Durban Light Infantry. The account of the incident was published in the *Morning Post* on New Year's Day 1900 in the hand of war correspondent W.S. Churchill who, prior to being captured by the Boers, was instrumental in salvaging the situation after a 15-pound shell from the Boer's Creusot gun knocked out the naval gun after it had fired just four rounds. Endeavouring to make good his escape from the scene across country back to Frere and Estcourt, Mr Churchill, though unarmed, was confronted by a mounted Boer burgher and forced to surrender. Very few people realise when he made his wartime speech forty years later containing the words *"we shall never surrender"*, that he had once had to do so himself.

Estcourt is back in the news following a string of political attacks in the area which has a long history of political intolerance. In the 1990s violence between the ANC and Chief Buthelezi'a Inkatha Freedom Party left many dead. The pressure is again on the ANC with several councillors being attacked and killed in their homes, ANC Councillor Sibusiso Majola being gunned down in March 2013. Those accused of the recent killings are alleged to be members of the National Freedom Party, a splinter group of Inkathata FP. It is being made clear in the wards that ANC is not wanted. The ANC openly blames one political rival party for the killing of its members. The gun is presently prevailing over the Ballot Box. As the 2014 election year approaches, Mary de Haas, KZN violence monitor, considers it unlikely that tensions will disappear. With all three parties contesting the event, she expects tensions to increase. The people are of volatile temperament. The elections come 20 years after 'Democracy' and many electoral promises will be repeats of past intentions upon which delivery remains expected. The government has recently committed to providing troops for the intervention brigade operating under the auspices of the United Nations Organisation Stabilisation Mission. The brigade is designed to neutralise armed groups in such places as eastern DRC and CAR. According to Lieutenant-General Vuzimuza Masondo, however, budgetary constraint has crippled the SA Defence Force in its attempt to fulfil national and international obligations. The announcement of the effect of defence curbs comes as the ZAR touched a fresh four-year low of R9.5875 against US$1, the weakest it has been since April 2009. Labour strife in the mining sector, particularly at Anglo American Platinum where 6,000 jobs are at stake, is the primary cause. ZAR14.5868 : GBP£1 and ZAR12.2957 : €1 were also recorded.

Minister of the Police, Nathi Mthethwa, and the MEC for Transport, Community Safety and Liaison, Willies Mchunu, visited the area and met the parties to discuss the escalation of violence, particularly with a view to discouraging it before next year's elections. The hostility between the parties was perfectly apparent at the meeting. Obviously neither party accepts that any of its members are to blame for any atrocity occurring in the other. NFP and Inkatha leaders suggested that the Minister and the MEC had only turned up after ANC leaders had been attacked and killed. That was favouritism!

Meanwhile 20km south of Pietermaritzburg, residents of Hopewell blocked their main road with rocks and burning tyres in a service delivery protest. Schools were closed for the day and workers were prevented from functioning. Taxis lost half a day's revenue. The crowd that assembled were asked to disperse by police. When they did not respond, tear gas and rubber bullets were used. Residents of an old-age home were affected by the gas. How long before something goes as wrong at one of these incidents as it did at Marikana?

These reports coincide with the revelation that 30 youths have died in the last 9 days at initiation ceremonies that include circumcision in the north-eastern province of Mpumalanga. A further 6 youngsters died in Limpopo. The deaths are being investigated as murder cases. Preliminary indications were that the youths died of excessive bleeding and dehydration. No arrests have been made. It will be for the National Director of Public Prosecutions to make a decision on how to proceed. For a change the President was forthcoming. *"As we speak our children are being killed by old people during the circumcision rituals that are part of the tradition of initiation of young boys into manhood. Hundreds of thousands of our children in this country, and millions around the world, undergo safe circumcision rituals every year."* – *"There is therefore no reason to tolerate that incompetent individuals continue in the manner in which they have been continuing."* Zuma told the House of Traditional Leaders Initiation ceremonies are common in South Africa as a three-week rite of passage into adulthood. Some 30,000 youths had signed up for the initiation this year. These deaths occurred at government-registered initiation sites. The Department of Health had been alerted but only showed up after the first few deaths were reported. SKY News international reporter, Alex Crawford, succinctly commented mid-2013, *"the New South Africa is just like the old."*

CHAPTER X

INDUSTRIAL RELATIONS

'**SA braces for one of its toughest collective bargaining rounds**' cried *The Witness* as increasing labour unrest emerged as annual collective wage negotiations get underway afresh. These come in the wake of a number of hefty wage increases last year to end strikes. The annual migration of both the employed and the increasing jobless, meeting on the streets. The Director-General of the Labour Department, Nkosinathi Nhleko, is concerned that labour and bargaining organisations lack basic negotiating skills. This is bad news for the employed for they need the highest honed bargaining skills possible if wage negotiations are to be successful. The D-G wondered if some refresher courses in HR at business schools might be necessary. It is timely that Amplats announced the retrenching of 6,000 workers, a compromise on the 14,000 first suggested. Investors took the Amplats' compromise badly. The announcement implied that four shafts in Rustenburg would be made idle and the Union mine in Limpopo would be sold off. The Department of Mineral Resources threatened to revoke Amplats' mining licences. Mines cannot now be nationalised but mining rights can. The share price dropped 4.4% to R330 and the platinum price dropped 1.1% to $1,490.01oz. and continued to drop. Only three shafts will now be made idle and production will be cut by 250,000oz. with a further 100,000 for the next few years according to CEO Chris Griffith. Impala Platinum led the downward trend with a fall of 4.8% to R110. Gold producers also fell to R1427/Oz and shed a further $68.45 to mid-May. Gold Fields dropped 4.05% to a 5-week low of R60.10 after reporting a 60% drop in Q1 earnings. On a much wider international front the Japanese Yen slid to 11.15 : ZAR having been nearly 11% higher a year ago.

The mineral that will cause the greatest havoc from its forthcoming scarcity is palladium. Russia apparently has a crisis that could cause worldwide inflation. What if manufacturers of car exhausts could not obtain palladium other than from recycling old exhausts? 80% of the world's supply may be in jeopardy due to the depletion of Russian stocks. At the time of the last such scare the Ford Motor Company bought up all the platinum it could, leading to a fiscal headache when the price dropped. Palladium is 15 times more rare than platinum and 30 times more rare than gold. It was discovered just over 200 years ago by William Wollaston and named in an anagram of Pallas the asteroid, and Athena the Greek goddess who slew the original Pallas, the mythological Titan god of warcraft. 'Pallô' in Greek means to 'brandish', as in holding an assegai in a threatening manner. Palladium has the lowest melting point and is the least dense of the Platinum Group of metals. It is mined in Transvaal, Montana, Ontario and Northern Russia. Most of the world supply, and its congener platinum, goes into catalytic converters which convert 90% of harmful automobile engine gases into nitrogen, carbon dioxide and water. Much of the rest of production goes into jewellery, dentistry and electronics. What if its future scarcity should add 10% to the price of a car? Much depends upon South African miners.

The publication of the Farlam Commission of Inquiry into the deaths of 44 people as a result of an industrial dispute ending in a wildcat strike will coincide with the formal wage negotiation process taking place. Dr Elize Strydom (employment relations executive, SA Chamber of mines) advocated that the rules of engagement should be respected by all parties from the outset, the laws that govern strikes should be respected and that wildcat strikes on an *ad hoc* basis could not go on. Marikana changed that which had remained unchanged since the advent of democracy in 1994. The greatest change of all is in the mindset of overseas opinion makers. Alex Crawford said it on SKY News that night (16th August), "*Has South Africa learned nothing in the last 40 years?*" The rand then stood @ R8.2268 : US$1. It stands @ R9.830 now in mid-May, a 16.3% difference. The difference against the Euro was 16.53%.

The damage which occurred at Marikana deeply scarred the illusion of the 'miracle' that is the new South Africa. Healing will be a long process. The government is regarded as leaderless, corrupt and most likely to cling to what it has for dear life, good governance being a myth. Trade Union leaders point out on the evening news the enormous gulf between the take-home pay of leading executives in the mining industry and the paltry sum earned at the rock face deep underground. The President warns that industrial unrest will lead to greater unemployment. In the 19 years since 'Liberation' the diseases affecting millions of miners who have now retired from the mines in their mid-30s to rural areas, are exacerbated by HIV/Aids, deafness, radio-active induced cancer, and virulent respiratory diseases such as tuberculosis and silicosis.

To preserve operational margins, mines are forced to employ the cheapest and most unskilled labourers in any economic sector, says Professor Philip Frankel in *Sunday Times (*19/05/'13). He is author of the recently released e-book '*Between the Rainbows and the Rain; Marikana, Mining, Migration and the crisis of Modern South Africa*. Short-term contracted labour drawn from rootless migrants hired through labour brokers fill many a gap and their employment is not many steps from human trafficking and slavery. Organisational structure linking the poles of the organisation from top to bottom, are virtually non-existent. Labour procurement officers who neither know nor care where a labourer comes from or what fate they send him to. The workers' accommodation far from home is in an uninhabitable shack and competition exists for jobs, housing and women between local Tswanas and poorly educated Xhosa migrants. Those producing South Africa's most precious metals live in the worst rural slums of Africa. What you read is not aimed at anything but spelling out the realities of the current situation. This book is not a novel. It's real. Sharp!

Looking at our gardener's pay slip I note that he is getting a little more than the official minimum wage plus a little over Consumer Price Increase data, a free house, water and electricity. He has no rates to pay. If he worked in the agricultural sector his pay would rise 52% to R105/hour. Then I'd have to ask him for a contribution to electricity and rates as well as charging him for housing at the rate I could let his cottage out for. Having done those figures I find that he would be 127% worse off! Little does he know that his employer's pension is 'frozen' at source by the British government, that we have had a 28.5% annual rise in petrol costs in each of the last 5 years and that electricity now goes up 8%. The municipality took him out of 'agriculture' when they said our smallholding is 'residential'. They unilaterally put our rates up 260.4% in a manner that leaves a lot to be desired. The category they created apparently is not legal. We are watching developments whilst paying the old rate. Last week Judge Margaret Vector reminded municipalities in North Gauteng High Court that municipal services are at the centre of the quality of life of all citizens and that they should remember also that they are their servants, not their serfs. The judge appears not to like municipalities either!

Christopher Salmon said many years ago in a BBC lecture that, *"No society can long continue in health by merely paying for work which it cannot make satisfying. Because the Victorians regarded work in industry as necessarily hard and disagreeable, they made little effort to introduce tolerable conditions into mines, mills and foundries, and were content to think of industry itself as an economic necessity instead of an element in society."*

Look where we are a century later. What have mine owners in South Africa done to make mining satisfying or conditions of work more pleasant? One fundamental difference between British/European mining and mining in other spheres, is that of domiciliary location. South African miners leave their natural homes and travel long distances to their place of work. By and large the former live on top of mined land and in secure housing, viz: the coal fields of Yorkshire, Nottinghamshire and South Wales. The SA counterpart lives near the mine shaft in a tin shack, cooks on an open fire or improvised stove and probably absorbs just enough calories to sustain him through the next day. The British miner comes home to a meal cooked for him mostly on electricity, his wife having finished work at her machine in a textile factory a couple of hours earlier.

As to working 'in't mill', the textile worker has to be satisfied with R375 (£27.27)/week for it gives her just enough for basic needs. Occupation is infinitely preferable to wandering aimlessly around a hungry location depending for sustenance upon the charitable nature of friends and relations. The carrot and stick hypothesis asserts that the main positive incentive is money. The main negative disincentive is fear of unemployment. When emotionally disturbed and frustrated at not achieving higher goals, the worker can easily be manipulated into group activity bordering upon mass civil disturbance. It takes very little to trigger greater focus on grievances than upon what little is satisfying. An accident down the mine or broken-down machinery at the mill is often enough. One item affecting the micro-economies of labourers is 'PayDay' loans. It is often called having one's pay 'garnished'. Loans entered into for the bare necessity of food are repayable on pay day. Many have been taken out both in mining and agriculture in SA and by workers in Britain, sometimes at extortionate rates. Repayment of the loan plus interest on pay day again leaves the worker with little cash for basic necessities and the diminution of available cash for food of quality leads to poorer quality of food being obtained and soon the pangs of hunger manifests into workers waving sharpened pangas. Debt incurred trying to work one's way out of debt is one of the most difficult traps to escape from. They got hungry on the koppie (hill) above Marikana and they got hungry in the Cape vineyards. The angry demonstrations, killing, burning and looting brought its rewards. Just because seasonal labourers in the vineyards were so poorly paid @ R69/day and got a whopping 52% increase to R105, so did every agricultural worker in the country. Farmers finding their margins severely squeezed will tighten up on work ethics and facilitate natural wastage wherever possible. Many will cut the hours worked during the week. Scattered settlements of rondavels and labourers' primitive cottages will become as evident as abandoned crofts and settlements around the coasts of Scotland and Ireland, symbols of a bygone era when all was relatively well.

Between mining, textiles and agriculture one has a cross section of the country's sociological make-up of the work force. Amongst union members, some are a lot brighter than others and the turf wars are fought by the most astute. A quarter of a century ago and with eight years of the struggle still to run, the principal unions of COSATU (Congress of South African Trade Unions) and NACTU (National Council of Trade Unions) differed in their organisation but shared ideas. Since the strength of a union comes from the numbers of feet on the ground, or underground, many divergent needs and views got aired. Lonmin's miners at Marikana were aggravated by the fact that NUM was seen to be losing ground to AMCU and only one union is allowed to represent the workers. Whilst both unions listened to their members they were unable to convert what they heard into action that benefited membership. The rivalry between the National Union of Mineworkers (NUM) and the new Association of Mineworkers and Construction Union (AMCU) has been a big event largely due to only the union showing 50% + 1 being enabled to represent the workers. By the time the annual negotiating routine began only 35%

of Amplats workers remained with NUM, AMCU having taken the lead with 41%. Times are changing and recent strife has led to participation by both unions in present negotiations and in future bargaining. The Chamber of Mines proposes that high-ranking union officials should be removed from payrolls. Joseph Matunjwa (AMCU) Senzeni Zokwana (President) and Piet Mathosa (Deputy President) are alleged to have been earning R800,000 to R1.2m/year. They certainly were not rock-face drillers! The brightest representatives capture time on national television and column-inches in the press. Joseph Matunjwa is one such union leader who held centre stage in front of 8,000 AMCU members at the Wonderkop Stadium. His union had triumphed over the National Union of Mineworkers, their rival of 31 years, and they wanted them out of their Lonmin offices. During the week an AMCU recruiter, Mawethu Steven, was killed. The Menzeni twins were killed earlier by men looking for a NUM official. Everybody subsequently went back to work. A turn of the page that they are reading, or a switch of focus on the evening news, and they are changed from delivering their views to being recipients of the views of others on totally different matters. If it is bad news from a hospital it possibly crosses the mind that they too could one day be in hospital. However, thinking that far ahead is not part of the native psyche. If it is a taxi accident, they live with the fact that it is what could happen to them, and fate is part of daily understanding.

When workers at Bryant and Mays model safety match making factory at Bow in London's East end first went on strike in 1888, the rights of workers to dispute their wage and working conditions were seriously questioned by the law-abiding English public. Even worse the strikers were women hence the strike was known as the London match-girls strike!

Eighty-five years later the establishment of the trade union movement in South Africa heralded a wave of strikes in Durban. Two thousand workers at the Coronation Brick works downed tools after over three weeks of deliberation. The initial agitation manifested into 5,000 workers in three major plants striking for better pay and shop floor conditions. The agitation was not confined to employment. There was a political dimension too and resistance to the apartheid regime was growing. Just as at Marikana, Zamdela, Boland and Sasolberg, the demands varied greatly. Oligarchies and dictatorships have something in common. They are usually led by despots whose character has emerged from childhood insecurity, through manipulation to being spokesperson for a largely hidden political front. Rule is largely maintained by fear; fear of being dumped by the hierarchy and thrust back into the bush, or fear of brutality from such as Sharia law most recently shown in Mali. The loss of a hand or public flogging equates unpleasantly with job loss from high office.

By contrast, with leadership expressed by a small elite inner group, South Africa wants the world to know that political decisions are a reflection of the widely-agreed consensus of ANC opinion. Jacob Zuma catches a lot of flak for not coming across as a leader. He may be atrociously advised or reluctant to take advice on matters of speech delivery and self-presentation. Correctly fitting spectacles would go a long way to alleviating the latter. Zuma has the cushion of having been appointed twice as leader of what they incorrectly term the ruling party. Monarchs rule. Democratically elected leaders govern. Whatever is decided by the executive leadership of the party goes all the way to promulgation. A hiccup occurs when Avaaz, an apolitical international organisation of +\− 44 million members lobbies South Africans implying that they should not be so dumb as to let their President sign legislation (Protection of State Information Bill) that enables him to plunder the State purse. A signature was hitting the site every six seconds; 50,000 signed the petition within the first 48 hours.

When dealing with his C.15th nobles, Louis XI of France (1423-1483) used 'Divide and govern' as his motto. Maybe the Board of Lonmin considered that once there was a split between union representations in the mines, they might be able to coerce one union at the expense of the other. Judge Ian Farlam's Commission will report thereon. P.W. Botha's National Party government went to great lengths in its efforts to contain and even crush COSATU, culminating in the infamous bombing of Cosatu House by State agencies in 1987. COSATU more recently have called the ANC to order on many fronts, particularly on corruption. With 69% of South Africans believing that corruption is on the increase in 2013, COSATU may have to raise their voice if they wish to be heard as loyal members of the Tripartite Alliance. President Mbeki would like to have copied Mrs Thatcher in neutering the trade unions. After Polokwane, President

Zuma continued the ugly conflict in which *the machetes that have been unsheathed and the guns that have been cocked in union land*, to quote Mondli Makhanya (*S. Times*, March 10) are not for battles over policy decisions, but *for the purpose of fighting about an individual who has developed a personality cult and whose conduct is the antithesis of what COSATU stands for* – Jacob Zuma. Worker's interests are likely to fall by the wayside as the President smiles smugly whilst leaning on the door of his taxpayer-funded Nkandla homestead admiring his cows.

As theology gives clerics a platform for discussing divinity, so trade union members collect to discuss their lives. Disagreement over divinity has led to diverse religious followings. Disagreement with working conditions led indirectly to the massacre by South African Police Service (SAPS) elite forces to the curtailment of the lives of 35 union members in a matter of seconds. The die was cast. Employers had to manage industrial relations better. The police required professional training.

George Elton Mayo, professor of Industrial Research at the Harvard Graduate school of Business, 1926-1947, said during his Hawthorne experiments with the Western Electric Company (1924-7) for the Bell Telephone system that, *"For their neglect of the human function of production, managers have paid a high price in strikes, restricted output and a vast sea of human waste."* The Hawthorne researchers demonstrated that there is *"something far more important than hours, wages or physical conditions of work – something which increased output no matter what was done about physical conditions."* Worker participation in change mattered significantly.

Doctor D.S.P. Robertson, of Unilever Ltd, reported at a meeting of the Association of Industrial Medical Officers that in an artistic fine drawing office containing some 20 men, old tungsten lights were changed for florescent units. Following the change many of the men had visited the medical department complaining of an assortment of symptoms attributable to eyestrain – such was the improvement in lighting. The trouble was resolved by consultation with the working group and it emerged that the new florescent lighting was only being made the scapegoat for other difficulties mainly due to faulty leadership of the group. It emerged that discontent was festered by the fact that the group was never consulted about the change before it took place.

At the end of April 2012 the U.K.'s International Development secretary, Justine Greening, announced that funding to South Africa would come to an end in two years' time. Ms Greening told a conference of African ministers and business leaders in London that the basis of future relations would be based on trade and not on development. Britain is entitled to be proud of the work it has done in partnership with the South African government helping the transition from Apartheid to a flourishing democracy. The current aid programme is currently worth £19 million/R266m per year. The South African government noted with regret the unilateral announcement that has far-reaching implications. South African spokesperson Clayson Monyela said, *"If you stop funding it means you stop the projects. That will mean that something will have to be done by government."* Maybe *something will have to be done by government*, but it is not going to be at the expense of the British taxpayer.

That which hits agriculture in the form of such a large rise in the basic minimum wage can be expected to hit other industries. Almost total confusion prevailed as wildcat strikes continued to cause five Exxaro-managed power station collieries to be idle for two weeks. The workers on strike were members of the National Union of Mineworkers and they have ignored a union call to return to work. Members of other unions were not on strike. The workers went on strike over non-payment of bonuses or performance incentives – unpaid as production targets had not been achieved. The union suggested that Exxaro might make an across-the-board payment. The company still did not see why it should pay anything for non-performance. They came back with a compromise single payment of 2% of annual salary [equivalent to R2,000 for each striker] on condition that the workers returned to work immediately. The proposal was rejected by the NUM without it being clear if they had a mandate from the strikers.

The only damage to property so far has been caused by stone throwing. Mining could recommence almost as soon as miners returned to work according to Exxaro. A slight misrepresentation of the seriousness of the matter which led to two trucks being hijacked in order to block roads while police are reported to have opened fire on 2,000 miners with rubber bullets at the idle Grootegeluk colliery, injuring some 15 workers.

The next phase was for the company to approach the Labour Court for an interdict obliging the workers to end their strike and return to work. Strikers have, in the past, blithely ignored such interdicts knowing that little or no punitive action would be taken against them.

Lack of service delivery or interruption of utilities is trotted out daily as the reason for some disturbance. The community of Nhlalakahle informal settlement protested against their electricity being disconnected by burning old tyres and throwing rocks at passing cars. They were angered by security personnel charging at them with guns. Some residents had lived there for 20 years and it was a long time since they had been promised electricity and improved services, but they have never been delivered as anticipated. An apology was issued by the ward for the damage to cars. Apologies do not pull or beat out dents and do spray painting. How long before such a situation ends with a fatality – or more than one?

It was considered perfunctory when the Deputy President accepted that the reason for AMCU not signing the wage deal for miners over the next 12 months was that union leaders had an obligation to consult their members before ratification. AMCU have recently grabbed a lot of power in the mines at the expense of the NUM. Thus it was all the more important that they should get the protocol right. Well, that was the reason given at the time. It transpired a month later at the end of July that AMCU members rejected the government's peace pact with members in the gold sector leading the way. Union Treasurer, Jimmy Gama, put on record that submissions made by the union were excluded.

The union demanded that Anglo-Gold Ashanti should reinstate 539 staff who were sacked for participating in an unprotected strike. Likewise 1,000 Glencore Xstrata employees similarly got the chop for going on strike over racism allegations. In quite a different field the union asked for Higher Education Minister, Blade Nzimande, to retract statements he was alleged to have made about AMCU members being *"vigilantes and liars."*

At the end of July the union still had to give the government the actual feedback from members about the peace pact whilst the door to the negotiating room remained ajar. AMCU, formed in 1998 as a breakaway faction of the COSATU-affiliated NUM, has come a long way in the context of that framework and understands well enough that when an agreement is reached the law should prevail. 'Turf' wars over membership in the platinum sector, is likely to emerge from the Farlam Inquiry as a contributory factor to Marikana.

The President has vowed to take a hard line against labour unrest in the mining sector. Was he motivated by recent eulogies to the late Lady Thatcher I wonder? Strikes and stoppages in the mining sector cost the country R15.3bn in output in 2012. The sector has a market capitalisation of R1.4 trillion – that's 16% of the overall value of the Johannesburg Stock Exchange (JSE) and therefore a significant contributor to the national economy. With a general election looming into view, is the President going to take a hard line against the miners? What percentage of disgruntled miners vote with their eyes closed?

One chilling warning often draws a riposte from the adversary. Joseph Mathunjwa, president of AMCU, emitted the warning that the country is being set up for a second phase of Marikana. It came in the aftermath of wage talks between the unions and the Chamber of Mines representing such major stakeholders as Anglo-Gold Ashanti and Gold Fields. Clearly apparent was the hostility AMCU faces from the ANC and the NUM.

Being called *"a cockroach that should be sprayed and eradicated"* is not appreciated by the union that has recently come to the fore as representative of the 120,000 mainly platinum miners in particular. A million people were eradicated in Rwanda a few years ago after they were called cockroaches. NUM still boasts 270,000 members with steadily declining numbers.

At the Commission for Conciliation, Mediation and Arbitration (CCMA) the NUM, Solidarity and **U**nited **A**ssociation of **S**outh **A**frica (UASA) declared a dispute. The Chamber of Mines declared a dispute against AMCU. Mr Mathunjwa could not see how CCMA could bring the parties together. UASA was founded on 7th July 1894, a century before the struggle ended with democratic elections. One of South Africa's oldest trade unions, their speciality is representing the interests of 74,000 members engaged in the diamond mining, motor, manufacturing, transport, mining and engineering industries. It would seem expedient to have such a senior union on one's side in any dispute. The schism between what the unions wanted and the 5% that the employers offered is gigantic. At the other extreme, AMCU sought a 150% hike in wages and the NUM 60%. The government announces its intention of using R1bn of taxpayer's money to settle the land claim over MalaMala game reserve. If it goes through there will not be much left in the kitty to settle all the other land claims in the pipeline for this year and that would be a major setback for land reform. The deal involves 15,000 people living in several villages 5km from Kruger National Park. Which claim should take government priority? The wages of 300,000 miners, or the claim of the 15,000?

Now what would you say as a miner in answer to the statement *"we* (government) *haven't got the money."* The Afrikaans "absolute *kuk!*" is one possibility. My late mother-in-law's '51ar' is another when you substitute the appropriate Roman numeral for the figure '50'. Government pushes for a R500m cable car on the edge of uKhahlamba-Drakensberg World Heritage Site but does not think that a rock face driller is worth R150,000/year. These sorts of priorities often face governments. The Minister who exudes charisma and has the ear of the President or Prime Minister is in with a good chance when he sees the head of government finance. Every Minister wants a share of the public purse to demonstrate how well the money is spent on behalf of voters and *"Deil tak the hindmost! On they drive"* said Scotland's favourite son, Robert Burns (1759-1796). He said it in *'Address to a Haggis'* a poem written in 1786 that has become the centrepiece of Burns night suppers. (25th January).

Notwithstanding the fact that Edinburgh is a long way from the SA Chamber of Mines, a lot of media reporting has gone into the 2013 annual wage negotiations. As a gold miner producing AU (scientific symbol for gold and the initials of the African Union), you find yourself supporting NUM whose opening offer was just 4%. The union described the offer as *'insulting'* and they know that they are not going to achieve the 60% increase that they seek. AMCU and NUM vie for pole position as do the likes of Sebastian Vettel, Kimi Raikkonen, Fernando Alonso, Lewis Hamilton, Mark Webber and Nicko Rosberg, the current top six F1 championship drivers. NUM has lost 80,000 members; the drivers dare not lose 1/100th second! The NUM is the most powerful member of the premier trade union (COSATU). It seems a bit like a game of dominoes which British miners play a lot, until it becomes violent. The deaths of three AMCU organisers in a Quarter in a country where life is cheap quickly became a statistic. They were senior organisers wearing their union T-shirt proudly. Members of an opposing union possibly chose to end the rivalry.

A 46-year-old AMCU regional organiser in the Rustenberg Platinum belt was shot four times in the back with a 9mm pistol whilst watching soccer with friends in *Billy's Tavern* near Shaft 2 of Anglo Platinum's Khomanani mine on 11th May. An assassination!

CHAPTER XI

ESKOM

South Africa's electricity sector contracted 1.2% in 2012 due to a buy-back programme and maintenance costs of ageing power stations. The supply of low-grade coal to some power stations further constrained power output. The country's best coal was going to China. China is determined that economic growth should not fall below 7% and that is a cause for optimism.

The power situation was so acute as we entered the winter of 2013 that the national parastatal was spending millions advertising steps that should be taken to minimise power consumption. These 'millions' came out of the pockets of the general consumer, not, please note, out of the pockets of the shareholders of large industrial corporations with whom Eskom contracted to sell power at a loss, nor out of the pockets of those government ministers who, failing to see that the country was growing, bought submarines, fighter aircraft and helicopters in self-enrichment arms deals.

State-owned Eskom Holdings SOC Ltd. is straining to meet demand from a growing economy as consumption is set to swell when the Southern Hemisphere winter drives the need for heat. 'Eskom' is the most emotive business name synonymous with any of the parastatals. As is often the case worldwide, Eskom is the sole national monopolistic supplier producing 95% of the nation's power requirement. The company is headed by a Board of Directors, none of whom has spent a day of their real working life in any industry associated with power generation or resource distribution, save for the CEO. Political intervention in times of trouble often ends with the short-out of a CEO of good political standing but weak in business acumen. Head office in Johannesburg is appropriately named Magawatt Park and it is there that CEO Brian Dames (pron. Dam'es) leads the board of nodding heads. Between them they took home over R13m for a few days' work in 2011. It would be wrong to trivialise the matter for, without a layer of management that produces some plans that enable the consumer to see after sunset, we would all go to bed a lot earlier, burn more candles and watch less television. After a long night's rest, more of us would get up with the sun and enjoy the dawn chorus of birds. But for a cracking good team at the end of the supply line in rural Underberg and Himeville, food stored in deep freezes would be thrown out with greater frequency on account of the long duration of power failure. The European wartime handover of the 'Blackout' is one of the changes that have been made with good humour. Eskom reminded customers in 2008 that since the end of the struggle and the advent of democracy in 1994, it had become politically incorrect to use the term 'Blackout'. Areas in which the power supply had temporarily failed, or had suffered from storm damage, should now be referred to as 'previously lit areas'!

"We do see a significant risk of power shortages." – Shaun Nel, director at the Energy Intensive User Group of Southern Africa, whose 32 members include the local units of BHP Billiton Ltd. (BHP) and Arcelor Mittal. (MT) *"We are seeing a significant number of factors that point to a system in distress."* Faults at a nuclear power plant near Cape Town are crimping supply, while imports are reduced because of flooding in Mozambique.

Paralysed factories would imperil South Africa's 2013 growth forecast of 2.7 percent. The rand dropped to a four-year low in May 2013, partly on concern that disruptions to mining will cut exports from the holder of the biggest-known reserves of platinum and chrome, and fifth-largest gold producer. The first Foreign Direct Investor to hit the brake pedal 2 years ago was Rio Tinto Zinc who cancelled a $2.6bn investment in South Africa for the building of an aluminium smelter at Coega, Port Elizabeth. South Africa's mining industry, backbone of the continent's biggest economy, is heading for its worst electricity shortage in five years in a threat to platinum and gold production and to the ZAR currency. In order to cope with the current (autumn, 2013) situation, Eskom has cut the power to BHP Billiton's smelters at Richard's Bay for up to 2 hours/week without compensation (in line with original agreements). Rather than invest locally, Tharisa Minerals has opted to build a ferrochrome smelter in

China instead of Rustenburg because Eskom could not supply enough power until 2018.

Now that the industry knows that the recent tariff hike was just 8% instead of 16%, the Intensive Users Group who account for 40-45% of the country's electricity, continue to point out what the hikes do for investment in South Africa. Chairman Mike Rossow expressed that his group had reached tipping point. He said that between 2002 and 2010, coal, oil, natural gas, metals and car manufacturing had attracted the lion's share of Foreign Direct Investment. As power consumption and tariff hikes increased, so the manufacturing and production costs in these industries rose. Investors build factories and create jobs. Stifle returns with higher costs and the investor looks elsewhere. At the World Economic forum in Cape Town it was said that South Africa was open for business and that the returns on investment would be good.

Nobody in government was listening when Rossow said that the country needed to be able to settle imports and exports through its balance of payments. The companies who had invested in South Africa were also the first companies that created the exports which earn the foreign currency necessary to pay for imports. Two years on and the trade deficit has ballooned to a point where the country will not be able to import the goods and services it needs to drive badly needed exports. Textile workers at Mooi River wanted a foreman removed and went on strike when management dragged their heels. Striking workers found the electrical transformer that served the factory and set it on fire. There was a delay in getting the power restored to the factory because some part of the transformer has to be ordered from overseas. Surely to God a transformer containing few moving parts except electricity current could be manufactured in SA?

Eskom targets spare capacity of 15 percent. Peak power demand of about 31,000 megawatts this autumn week compares with the more than 36,000 megawatts consumed at the height of last winter. One megawatt is enough to power 500 to 1,000 U.S. homes. Eskom, generator of about 95 percent of the nation's power, estimated surplus capacity over peak demand for March 18 at just 1.5 percent. *Sunday Times* suggested just one percent! That's as thin as the margin was when the power cuts struck five years ago, pushing gold and platinum prices to records as Anglo, Impala Platinum Holdings Ltd.

(IMP) and Harmony Gold Mining Co. (HAR) halted operations. By mid-winter the fears about capacity forecast were confirmed. As the winter solstice passed consumers drew 35,228 MW from a capacity of 35,788, a margin of just 1.59%.

An average of about 10,800 megawatts, or 25 percent of Eskom's total capacity including imports from Mozambique, has been unavailable this year because of maintenance, both planned and unforeseen, according to data from the Johannesburg-based utility. Eskom is spending $55 billion to replace old equipment and expand capacity. Faults at the Koeberg nuclear plant north of Cape Town kept it partly shut until April, while imports from Mozambique have been cut by 50 percent.

"*This winter will be a particular challenge*," Eskom Chief Executive Officer Brian Dames said in an interview on Johannesburg-based Talk Radio 702 on March 18. "*I am concerned about the increased unreliability*." Eskom said in a status bulletin yesterday that "*the system remains tight*." It is tight for Brian Dames too. Newspaper reports suggest that his term may end mid-winter when CFO Paul O'Flaherty leaves. Like his predecessor, Jacob Maroga, he is the only member of the Eskom board who has spent a day of his working life in the industry. The rest appear to be political appointees who took home just over R13m. between them last year.

Power failures may weigh on metals producer stocks. On Jan. 21, 2008, as Eskom reported, it was announced in July 2013 that Medupi is unlikely to produce any power before June 2014 and there will be none from Kusile for a further year. This could result in a 700mW (out of 36,000mW) shortage next year. Eskom has recently been down to less than 1.6% spare capacity. Frightening!

On the Johannesburg Stock Exchange Harmony Gold fell 4.9 percent, Impala dropped 6.2 percent and Kumba Iron Ore Ltd. (KIO) 6.3 percent. History may be about to repeat itself.

The Medupi project, a 4,800-megawatt, R91.2 billion ($9.8 billion) plant that was due to start output in September 2011, will be the world's fourth-biggest coal-fired station once complete. Medupi has been beset by delays, with labour unrest resulting in a two-month construction shutdown this year. The plant, north of Johannesburg is already running at least a year behind schedule. Labour unrest at Eskom fuel suppliers has added to concerns that generation may be disrupted. Wind generation of power is coming in the short term. Its arrival adds to the balance of payments deficit and not a single South African will be employed manufacturing the plant and equipment.

Strikes have halted output at 6 of 11 coal mines owned by Exxaro Resources Ltd. (EXX), South Africa's second-biggest producer of the fuel, and curbed supply to some of Eskom's power stations. The utility burns coal for 80 percent of its generation, and gets one fifth of its supplies from Exxaro.

"We're going to remain in a significantly strained power system until Medupi comes online," said Nel of the Energy Intensive User Group. And that's not going to be 'tomorrow' and it may not be 'next year'. Construction of the second coal-fired power station at Kusile was also disrupted by an illegal strike in the late summer of 2013. The government would like it to come on stream in the next ('election') year and has made it clear that it will not tolerate any more disruptions. It will add another 4,800-megawatt to the national grid. These projects are set to ensure that the country has enough power to underpin an economy growing @ 3%, 5% being more desirable when inflation is 6%.

"We are concerned about the impact which a sustained strike could have on security of supply," Hilary Joffe, an Eskom spokeswoman, said in an e-mail on March 20th. "We have more than 48 days of coal stocks across the system." That's more than the 39-day average at the end of March 2012, Eskom said in its annual report. In early March 2008, stockpiles at Eskom's 12 coal-fired plants ranged between 5.4 days and more than 20 days.

Grootegeluk is one of five collieries supplying three of Eskom's three thermal power stations which can continue to operate for at least two weeks. Industrial action had not affected deliveries from colliery stocks that could keep some of the power stations going for 30 to 45 days. Eskom is running on a very fine margin of production capacity to consumer demand. In early March 2008, stockpiles at Eskom's 12 coal-fired plants ranged between 5.4 days and more than 20 days.

Eskom has been trying to renegotiate the original contract with Billiton for four years following the blackouts that cost the economy around R92bn. The fly-in-the-ointment is the feeling by shareholders and analysts that successful re-negotiation of the deal that had 15 years to run would result in a significant drop in investor confidence in the country. Confidence in commercial contract sanctity in South Africa would be undermined.

Any successful renegotiation would affect margins in the aluminium industry and that squeeze would invariably lead to closure of the smelters with a knock-on effect on future electricity prices and jobs. Billiton directly and indirectly supports 15,000 jobs in Richard's Bay. Electricity supply has been highlighted by the leading credit agencies as a reason for downgrading the South African economy. If Eskom is now seen by international investors as trying to get out of legal obligations entered into in good faith, it could have serious consequences during the next round of credit assessment by those agencies. At worst, South Africa will suffer lack of investor confidence just when FDI is needed to shore up the trade gap as well.

The big Billiton rip-off was the headline of *The Witness*, South Africa's oldest daily newspaper, Est. 1846. As Eskom developed nationally and produced much more than was being consumed, it found a market for high consumption users in Industry and Commerce. One of the giants to strike an advantageous deal was resources group BHP Billiton. The contract was entered into in the early 90s. The Hillside and Mozal aluminium smelters then consumed about 6% of South Africa's generated electricity. The article revealed that Eskom was now selling 9% of its electricity to Billiton's two smelters at 20% of the tariff paid by other electricity consumers. The Supreme Court of Appeal had upheld *Media24* journalist's application to have the details of the contract revealed. Households pay about R1.40 per kWh, Hillside is paying R0.2265/kWh. A standard tariff of R0.228 applies to Mozal. It costs Eskom an average of R0.41 to supply one kWh. According to the most recent contract following the extension of Hillside, the tariff was approved by the Regulator (NERSA) on condition that other consumers should not be disadvantaged by it. Mines which also buy directly from Eskom and pay the same tariffs as industrial users are known as being on *megaflexi* rates which pay an average of R0.58/kWh.

And just as all this comes to the fore, the secret formula $ES \times 6.53 \times AL \times R/\$ = $ rand is declared where ES is the total number of gigawatt hours consumed in a particular year and AL is the price of aluminium on the London Metal Exchange. It is as important to the

South African consumer as the laws of space and time, $E=mc^2$, were to Albert Einstein (1879-1955). It was reported by Renee Voolgraff in the *Sunday Times* in early August 2011 that the information on secret pricing agreements between Eskom and BHP Billiton entered into in the early 90s must be released — but there might be an appeal... and there was. Judge Frans Kgomo said that the release of the information in contracts was in the public interest. The application was brought by Media24 and Eskom said it would not oppose the ruling. Aluminium smelters, BHP Billiton, studied the matter and appealed in the interests of its employees, customers and shareholders. Its Hillside and Mozal smelters consume about 6% of South Africa's generated electricity. The long-term contracts (to 2028) were entered into when Eskom had a surplus of generating capacity. Financial statements in 2009 said that estimated losses for the remainder of the contracts were R8.3bn. a figure that was recalculated down to R 4.7bn after renegotiation of the Mozal contract. Very low long-term electricity tariffs paid by BHP Billiton have been a point of contention since Eskom announced in 2009 that it would start to hike its tariffs by more than 20%/year to help finance its capital expenditure programme. In the latest round of proposed tariff increases with the National Energy Regulator (of SA), Eskom applied for 16% in each of the next five years and got 8%. New cost factors found on the consumer's tax invoice from April 2013 make up some of the difference. There seems no reason why:

a) Eskom should sell electricity to BHP Billiton for half what it costs to produce, and

b) Why the domestic consumer should pay Eskom R1.18/kWh more for the same power as is supplied to BHP Billiton.

The situation is plainly unsustainable.

A month after Brian Dames, CEO, said, "*This winter will be a particular challenge,*" the situation changed for the worse. **Winter blackouts warning** came with an exquisite photograph by *Witness* staff photographer of the sun setting plumb centre behind an electricity pylon. The warning stated that Eskom was prepared to introduce rolling blackouts this winter on some parts of the grid to prevent a complete system collapse. By mid-winter Eskom had already called on Billiton to temporarily turn off its two energy-gobbling aluminium smelters when electricity demand exceeded availability. Those who sail know the meaning of 'sailing close to the wind'. Too close and the yacht luffs head-to-wind and stalls. Eskom is very nearly there. The power crisis of 2008 forced factories, mines and smelters to shut down for days, costing the economy billions of dollars in lost output. The system is under strain five years later because of a massive maintenance backlog. Why not re-allocate the R602bn earmarked for upgrade of Sani Pass to Eskom to help clear the backlog? Oh, that would hurt those involved in the upgrade. Well I never!

The provincial government of KwaZulu-Natal is contemplating a 106m high statue of King Shaka at a theme park on the bank of the Tugela River at a cost of R200m. The site might be visited by a million people/year. The local government has been in talks with Dubai-based, Ruwaad Holdings who have presented a draft plan. You guessed it! Another import which the economy cannot afford; yet another project which will not provide a single job for a South African; except temporarily, when it comes to installation. When the story broke in *Sunday Times*, central government officials declined to comment. *Sunday Times* sought out the MEC for Economic Development and Tourism, Mike Mabuyakhulu, whose office is spearheading the project but even he could not be reached for comment. Eskom could use the R200m and thousands of statuettes of Shaka could be moulded, bronzed and sold at a profit – if there was a market for them.

Eskom is rarely out of the news and not always for the best of reasons. For well over a century a multitude of people in the developed world have taken for granted, once they got used to it, the fact that if they pressed a wall-mounted switch near the door of the room they entered, the room would become illuminated. Many South Africans have not yet experienced this long-promised pleasure.

This is possibly the time to relate how old houses were wired from room to room throughout Europe when electricity first became available, probably from the farm water-powered dynamo. Ferrets were in general use for controlling the rabbit population and they quickly home in on the smell of rabbit flesh. A carpenter drilled a ferret-sized hole in the woodwork supporting the wooden floor at each end of a room. A lad with fresh rabbit meat took up position at one end of the room. A hungry ferret wearing a collar with a fine line attached was released at the other end. As soon as the ferret found the meat the lad grabbed it, fed it a morsel as a reward and put it away in his basket. The electrician picked up the slack line and attached his cable to it. Signalling to the lad to pull the line that had been taken off the ferret's collar, the cable was threaded under the floor from room to room.

I am reliably advised that municipalities became suppliers of electrical power in urban areas in order to make money from selling it on to householders and commercial premises. Fine in theory, except for the fact that losses from cable supply theft ran into billions of rand. Msunduzi Municipality, controlling Pietermaritzburg, is one such case of a corporate body that sought to advise businesses and ratepayers in February 2013 of the proposed 18% tariff hike for electricity, 10% on water and 5.5% on all rates. The CEO of Pietermaritzburg Chamber of Business, Melanie Veness, told the municipality that the tariff hikes should not exceed those being proposed but not as yet agreed by NERSA. The municipality has faced a lot of problems through maladministration and corruption. The tide could be turning on what people are going to be told that they will have without guarantees that when they apply downward pressure on a switch it will have the desired result. When businesses throw the power switch they will want to know that 24/7, workers are going to be able to function with whatever electrical device their workplace is equipped with, PC or sewing machine.

And that's how Pan African chief economist Iraj Abedian saw things when he wrote in *Sunday Times* (24th Feb) "*Eskom has put a major question mark over South Africa as an investment destination and a place for doing business – it has also made a contribution to the country's credit rating downgrade*". Like it or loathe it, Eskom is nevertheless an extension of government. When things are quiet on the 'outage' front, the government is happy. When people moan about unscheduled outages and lack of service delivery the government becomes unhappy. At the end of April Africa's best read *Mail & Guardian* ran the headline: **ANC's hard road to 2014.** A survey commissioned by the ANC has revealed that there is a growing distance between party leaders and their supporters. A significant point coming to light is the fact that ordinary supporters are unhappy about the conduct of party leaders. Political infighting, corruption by party leaders and poor service delivery were highlighted. Bones of contention were the Nkandla

(President's home at taxpayer's expense) scandal, the perceived interference of the Indian Gupta family in government affairs (as civilians, they landed about 200 family wedding guests at Waterkloof military airbase, Pretoria to enjoy preferential treatment over resident citizens on 30th April), the Marikana killings, deep divisions within the tripartite alliance, the disintegration of the ANC Youth League, and the deployment of troops to the Central African Republic. The ANC relies on 1.4 million members to motivate the 12 million supporters who put them in power. **If the lights go out this time, they won't have any power, political or electrical.**

As to the man at the helm as CEO, he was the only Board member with experience in the power industry in 2009 when Eskom recovered from outages. It was Jacob Maroga. His resignation, or was it party recall, after 15 years followed on the heels of Chairman Bobby Godsell. His successor was Mpho Makwana, former Chairman of steel-maker Arcelor Mittal, who led a successful and complex turnaround at Eskom. His highest skills were in business strategy and his lowest were in board governance and strategic planning. He was also CEO of Saatchi & Saatchi and CE of the Marketing Federation of South Africa. Makwana has gone on to become Co-Chairman, World Economic Forum. Was it intelligent of someone in government to give him the push after just two successful years?

Two years on and they're after the blood of Brian Dames, again the only board member to have spent any of his working life in the industry that provides us with light and power almost all of the time. He is putting a brave face on looming outages and his departure from Eskom may come mid-winter when CFO Paul O'Flaherty steps down. The two played significant roles in stabilising power supply after the 2008 blackouts and in raising finance for development. The only project they have not got going without a hitch is the 4,800mW Medupi coal-fired plant at Lephalale, Limpopo. The site lies immediately to the east of the Waterberg coal field and to the west of the Mololo River, beside Eskom's existing Matumba power station. The budget has almost doubled from R70bn when announced by Brian Dames in 2007 and the starting date has slipped from September 2011 to June 2014, earliest. *"Even if they got God to replace Dames, He will still get into trouble taking on this job,"* said Mike Schüssler of Economists.co.za.

President Zuma should recognise that Eskom has caused much instability in the investment and business sectors partly due to government ignoring it as key to growth in the late 90s. Another round of heavy annual tariff increases is simply an indication that Eskom does not know how to finance the delivery of electrical power long-term. By making electricity more expensive, except to heavily subsidised large consumers on contract, the supplier is forcing the closure of many businesses. It has caused uncertainty with both domestic business and overseas investors and with a minimum agricultural wage of R105/day, employers are sure to pass on some element of their electricity bill to those workers that they house.

Fifty-one percent of remuneration received by CEOs of parastatal companies such as Eskom and Land Bank was made up of incentive remuneration. Eskom's performance was in recovering from extensive blackouts. The Landbank story is not without similarities. Mr Hadebe first joined the Land Bank as an interim CEO in July 2008 when he was seconded by National Treasury immediately after the transfer of the administrative powers entrusted by the Land and Agricultural Development Bank Act 2002 from the then Minister of Agriculture and Land Affairs to the Minister of Finance. Mr Hadebe joined the bank at a time when its finances were in a parlous state because of mismanagement, fraud and corruption. His first task was to lead the process of stabilising the bank's finances as well as implement the turnaround strategy whose main pillars were governance and adherence to the bank's core mandate. This was achieved and the Land Bank is today financially stronger and already plays its role in the development of the agricultural sector.

Returning to the old chestnut of Eskom's efficiency, there have been some simple lapses in management that have left a bad taste with consumers. In some rural areas Eskom sub-contracted the reading of meters to suppliers who simply ran off with the money. A tax invoice contains a panel that shows Actual and Estimated readings. Either estimates varied widely and consumers have suddenly had to fund R10,000 to make up the difference, or meters have been misread leading to conflict with credit controlling staff. Where a blatant error has been reported in quick time the error has been examined by an employed intermediary and subsequently corrected on the tax invoice. A minor upgrade of management might have averted the incident in the first place.

Once consumers could no longer rely on their meter being read promptly and accurately it became necessary for the consumer to report the monthly reading by cell phone to the call centre. Why, in a country where one in three of the working population has nothing to do and cannot find a job, the parastatals cannot train employees to do a simple job properly is beyond comprehension. Eskom runs a publicity campaign called the *"49m initiative"* The 49 million living in South Africa are supposed to back Eskom by saving electricity. It takes half a dozen e-mails, letters and phone calls to get a night-time street light that is on all day, attended to and corrected. In one instance the offending light was just 250m from the area office. It is reckoned that one street light on all day at the entrance to Underberg is left that way to reassure visitors that the one-horse town has power! Those who report such matters to Eskom or pass observations that might be beneficial to Eskom receive a terse e-mail stating that their complaint may be answered in 120 days.

In 2012 Eskom asked the National Energy Regulator (NERSA) if it could increase tariffs by 25.7%. Wise to the bluff, NERSA said that 16% was quite sufficient and at that time consumers still did not know to what tune they were subsidising the Energy Intensive Users Group. New consumers receive a booklet entitled *Eskom Info Pack*. The most reassuring statement is on the first of the 65 pages. *"NERSA ensures that electricity utilities conduct their business in the best interests of customers and for the long-term sustainability of the industry."* Is subsidy by the public of 9% of electricity generated and supplied to the largest users at a loss in the best interests of the other 91% of power consumers? I think not. I cry FOUL!

Minimum consumption occurs in the warmest months of the year and for the average domestic consumer of 1,000kWh/month, 38% of the Tax Invoice is for Network Charge, 31% is Service Charge and 30% is for actual consumption of power. A Retail Environment levy of about 1% makes up the total. At peak use during the winter months consumption rises to 57% while Network falls to 22.3% and Service to 18.3% The REL rises to 2.4%. C.E.O. Brian Dames said that Eskom really needed the 16% tariff hike that the National Regulator cut to 8%. My guess is that the National Regulator was neither satisfied with Eskom's case nor prepared to see the parastatals in greater trouble due to the hike being 2.7 times that of inflation and consumers having difficulty paying. When the hike was first announced the Pietermaritzburg-based Groundwork organisation executed a protest at Megawatt Park and found themselves in Randburg Magistrates' Court the following day facing charges of trespass, malicious damage to property, holding an illegal gathering and intimidation. The protest was due to Eskom's announcement that there would be further price hikes to pay for the new coal-fired power stations. Many well-intentioned revolutionaries all over the world have faced similar charges at some time.

Admirable as some might consider it to be for an electricity utility to be so well vertically managed that it produces its own fuel for power generation, there is a fly in the ointment. Coal mining and production at the pit head might best be left in the hands of those who know the coal mining industry well. As far as can be made out from the information available on the Internet, no Eskom director (serving or non-executive) has spent a day of their lives mining coal. Well-endowed as South Africa is in coal, there just could come a time when it is more profitable for a colliery to sell coal for export than to supply the domestic market. If the country comes to the point where it has to sell more coal overseas to finance imports, then a 'black hole' develops in the supply of coal to generate electricity. It is quite possible that some mines are already under pressure to supply export-led demand. The country's only anthracite mine appears to be selling high grade coal as low-grade anthracite. On a solid-fuel cooker or heating stove, anthracite neither smells nor smokes. Well, it didn't. It does now. High-grade coal is being passed off as anthracite.

Well, what happens if the mining industry goes for greater financial gain from exporting than supplying the domestic market? There is a power shortage and already butchers in Johannesburg have ceased storing meat in deep freezes. The 2008 blackouts cost the country R50bn. What's it going to cost this time…? All because a few years ago the governing party was so busy creaming what it could over an Arms deal involving redundant German submarines and Swedish aircraft that nobody had the time to look at what the country actually needed. Now there's talk of South Africa bolstering troop strength and becoming more responsive to improper governance in other African countries. A parody comes to mind; *people who live in glass houses should not throw stones*. Interference in the sovereign affairs of another country is unpopular yet the African Union chaired by President Zuma's ex-wife, Nkosazana Dlamini-Zuma, meets in

Chinese-built AU HQ to discuss how and where to interfere. The Central African Republic and the Democratic Republic of Congo are uppermost in their minds. Nobody would dare interfere with Uncle Bob (Mugabe) as the 89-year-old prepares for new elections, strictly democratic ones of course, monitored as 'free and fair' for all to see.

It is a critical call to decide which of the two concerns commencing with the letter 'E' matters most currently to South Africa. If the country does not have electricity industrial and commercial supply is interrupted, so are classroom lessons using computers. If the country does not educate the children now at school what are the job prospects of each year's matriculation? This very beautiful country inhabited by a lot of very lovely people has the potential to feed itself and most of southern Africa. Many of the native population have a high degree of integrity, the ability to work hard and enrich themselves as evidence of the burgeoning middle class and Black Diamonds shows. They are led by a number of lawless, self-satisfied, self-indulgent politicians bound in a congress for the purpose of capturing the state. The list of successes is short. It commences with the effect of extending widely HIV-Aids anti-retroviral treatment.

The list of failures is long:

- Inability to supply schoolchildren with books,
- Granting of government tenders to unsavoury individuals involved in corrupt practice,
- Appointment of key personnel to national jobs for reasons of political favour,
- Poor service delivery to deserving impoverished communities,
- Failure to create employment,
- Import of excessive amounts of goods that could be manufactured in the country,
- Enabling construction companies to build unsafe and crumbling houses,

- The inefficiency of Home Affairs,
- Spreading 'welfare' beyond the government's ability to finance it and other projects,
- Allowing the gap between rich and poor to escalate,
- Allowing teacher training to falter to the point of unqualified teachers giving lessons,
- Sub-standard hospital care as reported frequently in the media,
- Lack of proper training in law enforcement agencies,
- Too low a taxation base to finance the budget properly.

The ANC has the power to rectify all these shortcomings but lacks the capacity and the will.

CHAPTER XII

AGRICULTURE

Land Reform

The three-year-old Imperial British colonial government was going strong in 1913. The Anglo-Boer War was receding as a significant feature of the country's development and it was time to secure colonial land ownership by usurping the native population. Until recently tribal kings had played the role of the state and they were the owners of the Freehold. Warnings from far closer to Westminster were ignored. The Irish would do what Westminster told them, albeit under Home Rule. The difference was that Freehold of Irish land applied to everyone except Nationalist Catholics as had been long denied them by the Protestant Crown, and that issue was settled at the Battle of the Boyne in July 1690. 138 years later Catholic Emancipation rectified a lot of wrongs and it became a novelty for an Irish Catholic to own a piece of their own country.

The colonial government introduced the Natives Land Act, No. 27 of 1913 and that put 'the cat among the pigeons.' There were other equally discriminatory acts that became the cornerstones of later apartheid policy. In case the reader is not bird or cat-minded, pigeons seem to be doing well and there are many more fat domestic cats than thin ones. Agatha Christie coined the phrase with her 1959 detective thriller of that title. The scene was set from an English girls' school, the head mistress and a fortune of jewels that went missing in an imaginary Middle Eastern country.

The British thought that they could peacefully kraal the native population into just 7.3% of the country. Just as they had done to the

Catholics in Ireland, restrictions were placed upon the indigenous population preventing them from buying or owning land. Little wonder people denied their natural rights harbour resentment that manifests into revolution of some kind. Frustration overspills, the Bastille got stormed and the aristocracy guillotined. The General Post Office in Dublin became the focal point of the 1916 Easter Rising and dominant British forces hanged the martyrs, including a 16-year-old boy named Kevin Barry.

The Natives Act, 1913, made it easier for white landowners and captains of industry to recruit cheap labour from the reserves for exploitation in the mines and plundering the nation's natural resources. Migrant workers drawn from the Transkei to Gauteng have had to live in shacks to this day as a legacy. There is no doubt that the combination of historical displacement and appalling living conditions were features of discontent well before miners took to the Marikana koppie above the Rustenburg mine. Judge Farlam will no doubt comment thereon.

The Act also prevented white South African settlers from purchasing land in the Reserves to ensure territorial segregation of the races. Former Supreme Court Judge Sir William Beaumont led a Commission and travelled the country. He came up with a number of white-bias recommendations. His Commission doubled the land dedicated exclusively to the native population under the original Act. Under apartheid and particularly between 1960 and 1983, it is estimated that some 3.5 million natives were forcibly removed. It is possible that apartheid reconstruction of land ownership put the disposed figure closer to 7.5 million. Restoration of land rights looked a daunting task to President Mandela's first administration. [He was gravely ill in hospital at the time of writing.] Two years into his first term it was reckoned that 1% of the population (60,000), settled white commercial farmers owned a fraction under 90% of agricultural farmland. Of the 76,000 who applied to have land restored to them, an overwhelming 94% took the cash. The original target of redistributing 30% of the land by 1999 passed and the latest target date is 2014 due to just eight of the 24.6 million acres being transferred so far. The next year an impeccably dressed Native National Congress (ancestors of the ANC) delegation comprising Walter Rubusana, Saul Msane, Thomas Mapikela, John Dube and Sol Plaatje went to London to lobby King George V. The King was only able to pass their plea to his Liberal Prime Minister, Henry Asquith. The Westminster parliament backed the colonial government.

It is difficult to farm without labour unless operating as a wheat or barley baron of East Anglia, employing just one tractor driver or having ploughing, sowing, fertiliser application and harvesting done by a contractor. White farmers took advantage of the situation engineered by the nationalist government and exploited endless cheap labour. The worker that got R300/month in 2002 is now on R1,650. 'White' had to work with 'Black' whether they liked it or not in order for the farm to function. Modernisation and mechanisation reduced the number of native tenants of the settlers' land but plenty of them still exist.

As a sop to voters, the new post-apartheid government told the landless that the agricultural possessions that they had lost to earlier Nationalist governments would be restored. The 1913 Act was repealed in 1991. Anyone who had lost land under the 1913 Land Act could claim their land back. The closing date for claims was 31st December 1998. Land is to many what cattle, sheep, horses and goats are to others. The difference between land and animals is that it does not breed or grow. We cannot make any more of it. Just as one's first house purchase is a foot on the property ladder, so land ownership is the entry point of wealth creation. The only thing that man has managed to do so far to increase land is the drainage of Holland. By creating dams and canals the Dutch claimed back from the North Sea a mass of great agricultural land behind the Friesian Islands. From this northern region of Europe the South Africans gained their Holstein herds. The only difference to the eye between a Friesian and a Holstein is that the former should have totally white legs.

The 1913 Act gave white settlers from various European countries a platform from which to increase their wealth. The increase can be an illusion. The value of land cannot change except by astute farming. The higher the tonnage produced per acre, the greater the value of the land as a productive entity. What changes with the passage of time and of inflation is the number of bank notes necessary to purchase land. For example, the manor house and 500 acres of land in England and the mansion with similar land in Ireland that could be purchased for £9,000 in the late 1930s might have been sold for £300,000 in the mid-70s. The 3,233 percent gain over 37 years is an 87.4% annual gain in capital terms. Nothing physical changed on the land except for the growing and felling of a few trees. The hedges and fields remained the same. The most visible change was the substitution of a tractor for draught horses. Therefore it was only the money that changed value through its 97% fall in purchasing power. For every pre-WW2 pound it became necessary to show £33 by 1975. That's a different story to the illusion of land creating wealth. The only way to make meaningful comparison is to measure the two monetary amounts against an ounce of gold. It is the oldest monetary barometer. Its monetary value is set in London and New York every day.

The first government of South Africa's new democratic era said that 30% of white-owned farms should be transferred to native (black) ownership by 2014. They were making a promise to rectify the wrongs by land-grabbing colonials and national apartheid governments of the previous eight decades. The 7.3% of all South African land that had been allocated as 'Reserves' for the native (non-white) population had to be redistributed. Restoration of property/restitution of ownership was designed to restore land back to the original owners. [The author would quite like to have back the 20,000 acres that the Irish government of the 1920s and 30s purchased from his grandfathers but that is another story. A lot of Liffey water has since flowed through Dublin into the Irish Sea under O'Connell Bridge, the widest in the world for the span of water it crosses.]

The native population was invited by the government to lodge claims by 31st December 1998 for land that they could show that they had been removed from. They were given the choice of getting their original land back, obtaining alternative land if the original land had been developed for urban or industrial use or, opting for a financial settlement. The matter was not sufficiently thought through. An early poll of applicants with land claims indicated that just 6% of those whose families had been dispossessed actually wanted the land back in order to farm it in a sustainable commercial manner. The system was run by Land Claims Commissioners, one of whom, Tozi Gwanya, was a graduate of Leicester University in England. He became Director General of Land Affairs and as such was set up as the fall-guy for the slow progress of land reform. The system had become bogged down in spurious claims, poor offers, bureaucratic incompetence, and the allegation that when the government was a willing buyer, the landowner was not a willing seller. Expropriation loomed as a threat and the old chestnut came home like cows for milking – government wished to blame farmers for dragging their feet. Farmers pointed their fist (one does not point an index finger in Nguni culture except at close range items) at government failures to execute transfers timeously even when the price was agreed. At the ANC party conference in Mangaung, the President waded in saying that 'equitable settlement' must be substituted for the 'willing buyer – willing seller' synopsis. Nobody sees the difference! Only 10% of transfers have taken place and 90% of those once-viable farming concerns have failed. The farms have lapsed into disuse and disrepair thereby jeopardising both the livelihoods of the new occupants, and food security. South Africa has to import such basics as beef and wheat. It could feed itself and a few other AU countries if it wanted to. For the new owners, no material or technical support has been forthcoming from government. R30bn has been spent on land reform with little significant change to show for it. Some were able to get their land back without any visible means of cultivating or stocking it. A few years ago the Department of Land and Agricultural Affairs advertised a splendid scheme whereby a farmer could borrow 30 head of Nguni cattle for five years. Then he had to return to the government 30 similar cattle, keeping all that he had bred and the proceeds of sales over the years. If the Department's attitude to serious enquiries is anything to go by it is unlikely that the scheme got out of the feedlot, except in E. Cape.

Newly appointed Land Reform Minister Gugile Nkwinti considers that government has the ability to decide when farms are too big and how the excess should be distributed to native blacks. It is part of his Department of Rural Development and Land Reform programme commenced in 2010. One has only to look north to Zimbabwe where President Robert Mugabe's land reform policy bankrupted the country that not only fed the people but earned valuable foreign exchange from exports. Minister Nkwinti desires to see the remainder of the 140,000-strong community of white farm faces that now total 37,000, squeezed further. Excess land will be given to native black farmers. This is in the face of the fact, repeats Stephen Holland in *Sunday Times* (March 3rd) *that when 76,000 beneficiaries of land restitution were offered the choice between land and cash, 94% took the money."* The Minister appears to have no comprehension of economies of scale in agriculture. A 1,000Ha farm employing 6 workers @ R105/day costs R630 in wages or R0.63/Ha. The same farm employing 3 workers costs R315, or R0.315/Ha. If the yield per hectare is constant, the farmer will be better off with 3 workers than 6.

This Minister did an audit of the 26 million hectares of State-owned land and subsequently found 96m Ha. to be in private ownership. A significant part of the State's land is potentially economically viable. Distribution of this land would save the State the administration and administrative struggle of buying and transferring private land. So why does it not distribute State land and let commercial farmers continue producing more and more food?

Free bargaining has been used worldwide to assess the value of 'estate' and the most desirable prospect for a vendor is to have more than one person who covets their possession. Two people desirous of the same asset cause one party to outbid the other in an auction. Three in the mix and a real auction is in the making. When there is no bid at the first price offered by the auctioneer and he lowers the price in decrements until he gets a genuine first bid, the lot is knocked down to that bidder in what is known as a 'Dutch' auction. Minister Nkwinthi is charged with expediting land reform. His first quangos are the Land Management Commission and the Land Rights Management Board. The former is responsible for land registration and administration; the latter is responsible for maintaining social stability on farms. The types of instability envisaged are unlawful evictions of farm workers from their dwellings and illegal land invasions. No doubt the latter idea came from north of the Limpopo where octogenarian Premier Robert Mugabe has looked after his loyal lieutenants well.

When the means by which 30% of white-owned farms should have been transferred to 'black' ownership by next year (2014) faltered, white farmers were blamed for being unwilling participants in the 'willing seller – willing buyer' process in the transfer of land. Land is one of the most difficult things in the world to value. There was a time when it was reckoned that if it yielded 3%, that was adequate. £40 per acre valued the land at £1,333.33/acre. It was a useful yardstick of English values. Whilst they change over the years, the principle remains. How does one put a price upon one, two, three, four or five generations of tenants' dedicated labour, soil preparation and fertilizer? Putting back into tillage what the last crop consumed is one of the finer arts of agriculture, yet one too often glossed over.

The four pillars of land reform are now re-distribution, restitution, tenure and development. These pillars are designed to promote food security for that has been severely compromised by the ludicrously high failure rate of new farmers. They are designed also to remove the vestiges of apartheid and ensure that there is fair allocation of land irrespective of gender or race. The government abhors foreigners buying land to create golf courses and game reserves whilst natives are crammed into unhygienic shacks and makeshift structures seen on television whenever Marikana or De Doorns hits the headlines.

Mtobeli Mxotwa claimed in *Sunday Times* (June 23) that *"the country cannot afford to give land to foreigners to establish golf estates and game farms."* Well, it was the first time that anyone had read of the government giving anything to anyone except a senior member of the ANC, let alone any foreigner. Foreigners pay with hard foreign currency and this is the Foreign Direct Investment badly needed to shore up the trade gap. South Africa cannot have it both ways, however, much the government would like to redress the balance created by history. King Shaka welcomed the foreigners who came to visit him, accepted their gifts and was pleased to enrich the Zulus with their trade. If he had not liked foreigners he should have pushed them back into the Indian Ocean at Delagoa (Maputo) and Natal (Durban) when he had the opportunity. Maybe he should be blamed for the wrongs inflicted on the native population in two subsequent centuries? The Zulu armies under Shaka and Cetshwayo were strong enough as evidenced at Isandlwana. Maybe the colonial government of a century ago is not to blame any more than the Nationalists who administered apartheid. Blame it on that despot Shaka, I say, and that is exactly what his brothers eventually did. Out came the assegais and in his back they knifed him. Contrary to Zulu custom, they left him dead at the gate of his kraal until they buried him the following day. Despots are part of the African continent's way of life. If it is not Uganda, it is Guinea; if not there, Ivory Coast; if not there Mali or Zimbabwe. The purpose of the African Union is to try to stabilise the continent. Pretending that the last despot faces his last election, as with the case of Zimbabwe now, is not superior intelligence. It is a 'no-brainer' to guess that the precedent already set in so many African nations for so long will continue.

At the 2012 Mangaung ANC party conference, President Zuma re-opened the claims process. The move allows those who missed the December 1998 deadline to claim belatedly, thus further clogging up the administration process. It now allows those who were dispossessed BEFORE 1913 to lodge claims. This time aspirant land claimants will have five years to lodge their claims. The descendants of the Khoi and San people who lost land much further back in time are going to have a field day (pun not intended!). It is going to take a long time for land inequalities to be rectified and for rural poverty to dissipate. The whole process is fraught with conflicts of interest where great uncertainty and huge expectations have been created. Uncertainty has prevailed through the first 19 years of the Land Reform policy. As Freedom Front Plus leader Pieter Mulder said in the National Assembly during the debate on the State of the Nation address, *"Commercial farmers did not want to expand and so create new employment opportunities, because they were unsure whether they would keep their land."* Mulder went on to enquire if the Khoi and San descendants could reclaim land back to 1200, when those people were present across the whole of South Africa. Interesting!

There was an exquisite piece of writing in NO FRESH IDEAS, the heading given to the leader, *The Witness*, Feb. 18th, 2013. *"It is a major embarrassment that the very symbol of colonial oppression and Apartheid's looting of the birthright of blacks should be an orphan of democracy."* Coming from a country oppressed by an Imperial power for almost eight centuries, I am puzzled as to who feels the major embarrassment. Conquering powers gave land that they seized to those who had funded regiments and fought with honour. Neither Portuguese, nor Dutch, nor English had any quarrel with the Hottentots, Zulus, Khoi or Xhosas when they first settled. The prime conflict lay between the European nations who had established bases for supply and trade far from home. The English and Portuguese are amongst the world's oldest allies. The English said poetically of the Dutch, *"In matters of commerce the fault of the Dutch is in offering too little and asking too much!"* The Dutch are the architects of historical South Africa stemming from Jan van Riebeeck's landing with his wife, Maria de la Quellerie, at the Cape to establish a permanent settlement for the Dutch East India Company on 6th April, 1652. It was the Dutch who accommodated in their homes in the Netherlands the Protestant French Huguenots who were evicted from France following the

Revocation of the Edict of Nantes (which allowed them to 'protest' against Rome in Catholic France) – a right they were given in 1598. The Revocation came 87 years later. Their lives were overturned with many fatalities such as the drowning of 94 Protestant clergy at one time in the Loire by command of Jean-Baptiste Carrier (1756-1794). One of his methods was to put a large number of prisoners on a ship that had trap doors in the bottom, enabling it to be scuttled easily.

Giving the French little alternative but to learn Dutch, their hosts hand-picked the best artisans for transport to the Cape Colony. Two maps sold by the South African Huguenot Society show where the French families came from in France and where they were allocated as much land as they could plough in a morning around such original settlements as Wellington and Darling, Western Cape. The agricultural measurement of a morgens came into being as 1,000m² otherwise known as an Are and one thousand of them form a Hectare. As the Huguenots settled in and their numbers became stronger with further arrivals of shipments, so their influence upon Cape Colony spread, particularly in agriculture, including viniculture. The skilled carpenters of the time became wheelwrights and upon them, as much as upon teams of oxen depended the outward expansion from the colony throughout South Africa.

Mulholland enlightens readers further to the effect that a century ago 60% of those employed in the U.S.A. on land fed 76 million people. Today 0.7% of those employed do the same job to feed 320 million people and the country has a huge surplus to export. South Africa could take a leaf out of the American, Canadian, Brazilian, Romanian, French and several other national story books. The advanced farmers are importing foreign machinery to harvest larger extensions of planting. Mays, the local garage in Himeville, has just become a Massey-Ferguson distributor. Economies of scale in machinery utilisation imply that upon illness or retirement, a worker may not, in many instances, need replacing. The new national minimum wage of R105/hr. would have put farmer's wage bills up 54%. So farmers retrench whoever they can economically and cut the hours of those whose work can be done in a shorter space of time. Briefly, in the autumn of 2013, agriculture created 54,000 jobs as found by the Statistical Office. Wonderful if that could be sustained. Natural wastage means that in many foreign farming communities, one highly skilled tractor driver is drawing three or four times his predecessor's wages, working much seasonal overtime and enjoying a quality of life not previously experienced by agricultural labourers. It will not be long before the 2,500Ha South African farm with a payroll of labourers and hangers-on amounting to some 20 head will cut their numbers by 50% and reduce the wage bill by 40%. As yields increase and prices remain relatively stable, the farmer can be expected to modernise continually as now non-farm payroll numbers escalate. This is against a background in which the anthracite the farmer burns on his domestic cooker has doubled in five years and petrol for his SUV has done likewise.

It appears not to have crossed Minister Nkwinti's mind that crop failure in Zimbabwe due to non-farmers producing nothing is a real blessing to South Africa. The country has the scope to feed itself well and to export widely to the rest of Africa, its prime market. Investment doubt, security of tenure and political uncertainty is a mix that does not motivate South African farmers to go far beyond seeing that their families are all right, and if there is a surplus of wool in the market it will go for export and that will pay for another season's polo.

Twenty teams contested the GWK-sponsored three-day tournament hosted by Underberg polo club. No effort was spared to have the grounds in immaculate condition, all the polo ponies well rugged up overnight, the clubhouse in pristine condition, the bar well stocked and excellent catering. The visiting ladies of Royal Canadian Mounted Bears, members of Calgary Polo Club (Est. 1890) were beaten 8-4 by the South African Ladies Invitational team. Polo was first played at Underberg in 1894. Just a pity that the crowds of five to ten thousand who attended American polo in the 1930s could not be there.

Reopening the cut-off date for land claims to attract more claimants and pushing aside the 'willing buyer – willing seller' mechanism in favour of 'equitable settlement' is simply changing hues of the same autumnal leaf colouring. The statements surrounding these proposed changes have the hallmarks of a governing party tinkering instead of making changes to benefit the people and to ensure food security. The massive number of changed-hands farm failures bodes badly both for the people who took on the farms being able to feed themselves and they certainly are unlikely to produce any agricultural surplus for sale to an export market. Land claims prior to the 1913 Land Act will be re-opened. This may give high expectation to a few and it gives them a bone to chew whilst awaiting development. It should be remembered that in the old Zulu tradition the local leader held the land and those who wanted some for pastoral use applied for and received his authorisation. Neither freehold nor leasehold as we know it had been heard of.

Brian Habana, 2007 rugby player of the year and the only man to score three tries for the Barbarians against the All Blacks (Twickenham, 2009) is descended from the Gqunukhwebe Chief of that name who, with Chief Chungwa, raided and burned Cape frontier Xhosa farms that the Khoi had lost. Some of them still want their land back. The All Blacks had not lost a match in the Northern Hemisphere for two years. The Springboks played better against the tough Samoans than they had for several matches. Even the Proteas are excelling themselves on the cricket field. Both teams are captained by a de Villiers.

Only a very few who can trace their ancestry to a specific plot of land want to farm it commercially. The last figure mentioned was 6%. Cash in compensation for a loss a century ago is much more attractive. Cash buys 'lifestyle', food and drink and with adult life expectancy growing 11 years in the last eight due to increased anti-retroviral treatment, the cash might run out too soon, according to the UKZN Africa Centre for Health and Population Studies, 2012. Until ART became widely available in rural areas of KZN, people were dying in their 30s and 40s. Now they are living until pension age and beyond according to a further report by Jacob Bor of the Africa Centre and Harvard School of Public Health. And, the more that live longer the more that become dependent upon the State, and upon Eskom.

Weighing heavily on rural minds is the 52% rise in the agricultural minimum wage and how it came about. Thousands of people who have no regular job flock to the Western Cape for the fruit picking season from all over the rest of Southern Africa, especially Zimbabwe, Lesotho and the Eastern Cape, just as they do in Europe for the wine collecting season. It is one of the few sectors of the economy that employs unskilled labour. As Democratic Alliance leader Helen Zille wrote, "*This is fertile ground for exploitation. And it is easy to see how the dominant (but entirely misleading) narrative arose: 'Heartless white farmers and labour brokers make super profits by using divide-and-rule tactics to drive down workers' wages as their lives deteriorate.' It is easy to see how this narrative fuelled the rage that led to the destruction of tens of millions of Rand worth of farm infrastructure."*

The workers protests started on a farm called Kuerboschkloof where workers were paid above the minimum wage of R69/day. Pierre Smit, the farm owner, died and his farm was taken over by a Black Economic Empowerment consortium who immediately cut workers' wages from R14.50 to R10.60 per hour. Pay-day loans also featured significantly in the lives of these seasonal workers. Having repaid their loan from their pay packet there was little left for living, let alone eating properly. Understandably the workers protested. A former ANC councillor who is also a labour broker tried to bring in scab labour at the behest of the consortium to replace the protesting labourers.

Unrest spread to the Royal Mushroom Farm and to Normandy Farm with agitation by ANC always present. The Minister of Agriculture, Tina Joemat-Petterson, visited the area but to no avail in trying to calm matters down with inflammatory language. Wages are a matter for the Department of Labour and that Minister, Mildred Oliphant, remained abroad for weeks despite having set the minimum wage levels that were the subject of protest in consultation with COSATU. There remains a lot to be sorted out and traffic on the once-blocked N1 near De Doors is moving freely again. The ANC would still like the farmers to be known for their intransigence when the reality is that most farmers pay significantly higher than the minimum wage. They are struggling to make ends meet because of the low return on their product. Hex Valley table grapes sold in the U.K. provide the supermarket with a 42% margin whilst 32% goes to distributors and only 18% of the final retail price is retained by the farmers. When she returned from her parliamentary portfolio committee jaunt and joined the negotiations, the Minister for Labour applied the new R105/day minimum wage negotiated between farmers and unions, who had wanted R150/hr, throughout South African agriculture with effect from 1st March 2013. How a seasonal worker dispute in a specific location of viticulture came to affect the entire agricultural sector is difficult to comprehend. It excluded non-agriculture workers such as gardeners unless the land they worked on was termed 'farming' by the Revenue Services.

This resulted in the Department of Labour having to process 1,432 applications from farmers seeking exemption from implementing the government's 52.2% minimum wage rise. 41.3% of the applications were from farmers in the Western Cape wine growing area on the grounds that they could not afford to pay R105/day per worker. 20.3% of the applications from farmers were from far-off Mpumalanga province, the big cattle country between rich urban Gauteng and impoverished Swaziland.

That which hits agriculture in the form of such a large rise in the basic minimum wage can be expected to hit other industries. Almost total confusion prevailed as wildcat strikes continued to cause five Exxaro-managed power station collieries to be idle for two weeks. The workers on strike were members of the National Union of Mineworkers and they have ignored a union call to return to work. Members of other unions were not on strike. The workers went on strike over non-payment of bonuses or performance incentives – unpaid as production targets had not been achieved. The union suggested that Exxaro might make an across-the-board payment. The company still did not see why it should pay anything for non-performance. They came back with a compromise single payment of 2% of annual salary [equivalent to R2,000 for each striker] on condition that the workers returned to work immediately. The proposal was rejected by the NUM without it being clear if they had a mandate from the strikers.

In common with the Irish Land Act, 1923, the Native Land Act, 1913, appears likely to be the focus of attention for some time to come. In Ireland most land was distributed to the many existing tenants that remained after various emigrations during C.19th. Most were well mentored by the former landlord and many a glass of whiskey was downed as the mentor discussed practices with his former tenant. A high proportion of transfers succeeded to the mutual satisfaction of both parties. The South African government knows the Irish story. It is not in the nature of the indigenous people to replicate other people's success stories or examples. They would rather do it their way and if it does not work, well that's life. The South African has a preference for "moving on" from a fatal accident, family bereavement following crime, natural disaster, loss through corruption, a business failure or gross negligence as though nothing had happened or there was nothing to be learned. To their credit they seek the advice of the ancestors instead.

"*To err is human,*" said Mae West, after Elbert Hubbard (The American Bible) in 'The Wit and Wisdom of Mae West'. "*Experience is the name everyone gives to their mistakes,*" said Oscar Wilde in 'Lady Windermere's Fan'. "*If you live long enough you'll make mistakes. But if you learn from them, you'll be a better person,*" said Bill Clinton. South Africans may have learned from Yergeny Zamyatin's 'Contemporary Russian Literature', "*I prefer being wrong in my own way to being right in someone else's.*" The Russians eyed South Africa with communal interest. Collective responsibility masks many government decisions and it prevents a lot of people being brought to book for personal misjudgements, particularly in the field of politics and civil administration. The modern nation is less than two centuries old. The man wearing a smart jacket and trousers, shirt with necktie walking in clean shoes along the road in his 'Sunday best' is just four or five generations from the pastoral warrior who knew no roads, walked barefoot and wore a girdle of leather. The speed with which the South African indigenous native, especially the Zulu, has transformed him/herself over such a short period of world history, without being involved in international war, is truly remarkable. Given proper education the people will advance even faster. The decade-old U.S. Emergency Plan for Aids Relief (PEPFAR) programme to create an Aids-free generation has celebrated its 10th anniversary with the millionth Aids-free baby being born. Thus, infected mothers are giving birth to babies that will survive in place of both dying at some stage.

The benefit from reading this text book of a revolution is that the reader feels enormously enriched by learning so much about the people and the country they live in. The country's President is Zulu, the language spoken by 1-in-4 of the population is Zulu. That is three times as many who have English as their first language. When one flies from London to Rome, one travels to a much older city. From London to New York one finds a much younger city. A flight from Durban to Dubai takes one from $C.19^{th}$ to a $C.21^{st}$ emporium. Landing in Cape Town or Johannesburg (O.R. Tambo) from almost any city in the world brings the traveller into the world of the fastest maturing people found anywhere. First stop for many are battlefield tours. The battlefields are unchanged. Many visit game parks and reserves. The wild animals are unchanged. By contrast the people are changing as fast as cars and communications. When they stop to think instead of 'moving on' they will become innovative and make greater marks in the worldwide achievement. Just one fly in the ointment. The government may not want too many to gain the ability to stop and think. That's a pity.

As if farmers had not encountered enough difficulties in getting to the land that they now farm and cannot be absolutely certain that they will be able to continue to do so, there was trouble at Muden, KZN. Much is made of how people got their land in many countries, whether as a reward for valour in battle, or as a result of government policy as in the resettlements during the apartheid era. It is puzzling to some, how the Nationalist government plotted and planned without too much foresight. 'What goes around comes around' is an old lyric set to music by Justin Timberlake. The morals are many. We reap what we sow. Land claims will not be satisfactorily resolved for another generation.

The trouble at Muden not only affects farmers and wholesalers but school children and teachers. Anything that disrupts education in the country needing it most (140th of 144 nations) is a crime worthy of the attention of law enforcement.

A land dispute between a local farmer and the community has been referred to Court and MEC Willies Mchunu sent senior officials to urgently attend to the matter. Meanwhile the Muden community blockaded the R74 to Greytown with huge rocks making it impossible for farmers to take produce to market. Kwanalu, the provincial Agricultural Union, appealed for freedom of movement where the rights of people were infringed and there was no freedom of movement. The criminal act of digging a hole in the road has been overlooked by SAPS.

CHAPTER XIII

HUNTING

It would be surprising if early hunting was not mentioned here by an author who has hunted six furred quarry, and as many feathered ones, on two continents with 28 different packs of hounds. Some 20 quarry species roamed the plains, riverine valleys and woodlands of Zululand before the white man came with his gun and extensively extended his liking for antelope venison. The country was a hunters' paradise with no fences and no horses needed to jump them. It was all done barefoot. There was no 'close' season. Anyone could go hunting whenever he wanted, Sorry, no ladies. *umNumzana*, the district headman, was free to call a public hunt (*iNqina*) whenever he liked. This was the era of King Shaka; the coastland was very sparsely populated and jackal were a menace.

The hunt was as systematically and formally arranged with small exceptions as that experienced in European hunting. The English like a stirrup cup of good cheer before moving off from the Meet. The Zulu sings and dances. They don't need a Hunt Ball! The Meet was called by *umTónga* entering neighbouring kraals and crying loudly, "*Mé!*" as a Buck and announcing the venue on the morrow. The caller was not allowed to speak with anyone around the kraal for he might impart his own possible good fortune in hunting to another. On the eve of hunting people slept on one side of their body. If they turned over in the night it might impart restlessness in the quarry.

Following breakfast on a coarse, cold porridge, the hunters entered the cattle fold and prayed to the ancestors (forefathers) for protection and good sport. Similarly in Normandy and Central France on the Féte de St. Hubert (Patron Saint of hunting) a few couple of hounds were taken up the nave of the local chapel for blessing by the priest. The Zulu, praying for a buck that would not be too difficult to catch, Zulu hunting was a form of traditional battle with the beasts. The hunting 'field' formed up as for battle, a 'chest' and two horns. Each hunter carried a bundle of Assegais, a hunting shield (*iHubelo*) and a knobkerrie (*iWisa*). Just as it is good to see as good omens for the day the hedges looking dark on the way to the Meet in England, and hounds there fidgeting restlessly about the huntsman's horse, so the Zulu reckoned with good hunting if he saw a Redwing Francolin (*Francolinus levaillantii*) on his way to the draw. Should he spot *uChakide* (*Galuella pulverulenta* – small grey mongoose. Others say *uChakide* is *Mungos mungo* – the banded mongoose) he might just as well have stayed at home. If they managed to kill it, then the bad omen would be reversed.

As with formal European hunting, the Master stood in the middle of his associates at the Meet whilst the hunters kept to their kraal groups. A 'Captain of the day' (*umPáki*) with good hunting experience was appointed and they all sang the likes of *D'ye ken John Peel*, or, as the Wren boys in Pagan Ireland did many years earlier, after hunting the little Wren on St. Stephen's Day (26th Dec.), they asked in a ballad for the Mistress of the house to come out and give them a treat. After the singing and dancing, *umPáki* gave the groups their directions upon where to go and what to do. [This would be the same as the huntsman telling his whippers-in and a few hunt members where to go 'on point' at a covert to view away the fox that hounds were most likely hunting.]

As the 'field' departed the Master knelt down, plucked a bunch of grass with each hand and, putting one in his mouth he stooped low to the ground with his mouth as though grazing. With his hands he made a swishing movement whilst crying, "*Mé!*" The hunters responded every time, "*Ji,*" (as in French). The Master then threw the bunches out to each horn and sent them about their work, chanting their hunting song on their way. This practice also existed amongst the far-off Cape Xhosas.

When the hunter's assegai struck a beast he cried, 'Mine!' in the form of, "*Mámo i Nyamakagia*" plus the name of his kraal. If the strike was not fatal and a member of another kraal group landed a second assegai, or his dog secured a hold on the beast, he too shouted his own kraal's *isiGá*! If still a *runner* and a third person dealt the *coup de grâce* he shouted his party's *isiGá*. The first one who struck was entitled to the beast less a haunch to the second and a shoulder to the third.

Just as they do in Europe, all returned to the Meet and laid out the bag before the Master. He tapped a carcass with his stick and called for the claimant. If nobody claimed it the Master made off with the beast. If several should claim and the Master is unable to settle the dispute, he still went off with the carcass, his perk for the day. In Normandy in 1962 the 'field' of the 'Echos de Perche' wild boar hunt repaired to the Auberge de la Tête au Loup with hunt members for a superb dinner on the filet of the young boar caught and killed in the open between two parts of the forest. The Zulus that evening, or the following day, also participated in a feast. After eating they patted the hearthstones and prayed to the ancestors that the next hunt would be even better.

When hunting took a more serious form in the pursuit of dangerous animals, precautionary measures were called for and the *Sangoma* attended the Meet with ample medicinal magic. Before being sent on their way by the Master the hunters formed a circle around the *Sangoma*. He sprinkled each man with an Asperge of his own prophylactic, front and back, body and legs. For an added piece of luck each hunter thrust his assegai into the smoke of a fire sprinkled by the *Sangoma* with more potent mixture.

As to 'Royal' quarry, the English Crown retains the right to ownership of all unmarked mute swans in open water, but the Queen only exercises her ownership on certain stretches of the Thames and its surrounding tributaries (Swan Upping). This ownership is shared with the Vintners' and Dyers' Companies, who were granted rights of ownership by the Crown in the 15th century. In Zululand elephant tusks and the skins of leopard, lion, Cape ratel and the South African weasel (iNyengelezi) were all 'Royal' property. The Cape ratel (honey badger – *Mellivora capensis*) was much feared despite its small size. It had a habit of rushing in such an awkward manner at a man's feet that he could easily fall over trying to escape. The ratel went for the exposed genitals of a man, scantily clad in a skin girdle, who fell with occasional fatal consequences. Gus Mills records in 'The Complete Book of SA MAMMALS' that a honey badger reputedly attacked a wildebeest and a waterbuck by going for the scrotum. Both animals were believed to have died from the wounds.

During the threshing of oats, barley and wheat (generic English 'corn') workmen would tie a piece of binder twine around their trouser leg below the knee just in case a rat, concealed in the straw sheaves of the rick, should bolt for the dark hole formed between trouser and leg.

The reedbuck (*Redunca arundinium/iNtlangu*) was wont to die near water however small the pond. The red stag of Europe will even head for the sea when pursued under hunt pressure. If the reedbuck should fail to make it to water and dies in the veld, the *Sangoma* will find useful medicine below the spot. Hence the carcass was never taken into the kraal before the women were called out to meet it. The women left it to the men to take the beast into the kraal lest they bear children with permanent blue eyes (Native babies being born with blue eyes anyway!).

The kings and commoners of the Nguni people occasionally found hunting a good means of ridding society of disagreeable persons. A 'treacherous' or 'conspiracy' hunt was organised with the only prescribed 'game' on the card being doomed individuals.

Every Zulu man was by birth a hunter and some became very professional (*iPisi*). Trapping was widely practised with large straight-sided pits (*iGébe*) big enough to hold an elephant, covered with foliage. Other pits (*iVéku*) contained vertical pointed stakes upon which the animal became impaled when it fell in. The Zulus were just as adept with snares and traps, remembering that they had no wire. The pattern of hunting has of course changed from olden times described above. *Canis Africanis* (some would say the cross-bred mongrel) has developed into all sorts of shapes and sizes with particular emphasis upon the ability to pull down a reedbuck. In Britain the lurcher has been bred along similar lines, the true Norfolk lurcher being the cross between a coursing Greyhound (one of the oldest pure breeds in existence) and the collie (which probably arrived in Britain with the Romans, 55 B.C.). The greyhound produced the speed and the collie gave instinct to 'herding' the hare to the closest running mate. The first lurcher that the author owned was a cross between greyhound, deerhound, collie and whippet, a really versatile hunting companion. Currently hunting in Zululand and Natal takes the form of a Meet being arranged on cell phones and running dogs being brought in vehicles to the land of an unsuspecting farmer late on a bright moonlit night or in the early hours of the morning. The native hunters scour the veld for buck and when one is run down great credit is given to dog and owner, the former being worth thousands of ZAR. Betting will also have taken place on the side and large sums (to the poor anyway) will have exchanged hands. Alas, the veld is well watched by farm workers and little time elapses before the local Community Watch is able to broadcast to interested and affected parties how many hunters there are and their precise location. When the hunters realise that their illegal activity is likely to be curtailed by police and farmers, their greatest problem is to get themselves and their dogs quickly onto a public road upon which walking a dog is perfectly legal. It is the practice of farmers and security firms controlling the area to ask the hunters why all their dogs should not be shot. There have been incidents of the hunters themselves being in possession of firearms for the purpose of intimidating farmers. Many first-class running dogs have been destroyed in these circumstances on the pretext that the hunt was illegal.

One day's hunting with rifle that did not turn out beneficial to the hunter was that of one McIntosh Polela, spokesman for the Hawks, the crime investigation unit spawned from the Scorpions anti-corruption unit. Colonel Polela went hunting for reedbuck one day on The Swamp, a KZN - Ezemvelo marshland nature reserve bordered by the Polela River running past Pevensey, a settlement some 10km from Himeville. There is some difference of opinion as to whether the Colonel first pointed his firearm at local farmer Graham Acutt, scion of the estate agency founded in Durban in 1851, or if Acutt's firearm was pointing in the hunter's direction. Acutt is the only man ever to have called The McGillycuddy of the Reeks a bastard in public. Clan Priest Father Denis McGillycuddy has some sound counsel upon such matters. *"Donough, those are the sort of people for whom a prayer would not go amiss."* In an unfortunate accident the previous year, Acutt's son, Roland, went on a 'call-out' of farmers to apprehend hunters with dogs. Told by police to put away a .375 magnum hand gun, he did so obediently only to have the weapon discharge the round that was up the spout through his back pocket into the back of his leg. He was still using a crutch six months later.

The sin of the Hawk's Colonel was to 'tweet' details of prison rape after Kwaito star Jub Jub was jailed. It took him months to apologise.

Meanwhile things did not seem too bad financially. He was suspended on full pay of R323,238.41 and could appeal the decision against being kicked out of the police service. He felt that being a Colonel in the Hawks was above the law and he could hunt where he wanted.

CHAPTER XIV

FINANCIAL MATTERS

FDI might become elusive for the largest continent of the Southern Hemisphere for much of it appears to be going towards the largest island off the coast of Europe. The only explanation I can offer, apart from relative progression of the races, is the different profile in which 'education' is held. South Africa is at last grasping the 'education' nettle. A young, flexible, adaptable and mobile workforce with a median age of 35, the lowest in Europe, attracts foreigners despite Ireland's geographic remoteness. According to an EU Benchmarking Global City report, Dublin ranks as the best city in the world for human capital (HR). As a result of severe recession following a banking-building crisis, Ireland is one of only three countries in the EU where nominal labour costs have fallen. The people woke up to the reality that they might have priced themselves out of the market. Commercial property rents have halved in five years. Owners realised that they had priced themselves out of the market. Large user electricity costs @ €0.10/kWh have remained constant for five years. Climbing fast out of recession, the three most productive economies in the world have become Luxembourg, Norway and the U.S.A. Ireland lies 4th. If a small European island in the Atlantic Ocean can do it, why can't a country between two oceans?

As far as column inches is concerned, good and bad news are reported in the business sector of *Sunday Times* with equanimity. When good news exceeds bad, a sense of well-being prevails. When the bad news prevails, uncertainty and doubt creep in. The face with upturned smiling lips is eclipsed by downturned edges of a forlorn expression. After reading the two opposing columns one is left to one's own perception as to whether the nation as a whole is gaining or losing ground. As we are mostly born optimists or pessimists, that trait dictates our overall impression of the larger fiscal environment.

Finance Minister Pravin Gordhan has to fight his bad news corner on the World's Agencies (Moodys, Standard and Poors, and Fitch) downgrading South Africa and keeping its outlook on the credit rating negative. The Treasury suggests that Standard & Poors in particular *"did not take adequate account of the positive developments over the past six months."* Nobody in South Africa knows what these 'positive' developments are. Both Moodys and S & P downgraded the country last year, citing socio-economic tension, labour issues and increasing government debt. Adopting the National Development Plan launched by Trevor Manuel nearly a year ago at the Mangaung Party Conference and repeating it in the State of the Nation address a few months later are 'words'. The credit rating agencies are looking for action. What they see is what they find; a spiralling trade deficit, more police violence, the national electricity producer almost running out of power and the telecommunications operator retrenching 21,000 people. Be reminded, this is the country of the South African people, most of whom are 'black' natives. It's their business as far as they are concerned to run the country as they like and if it doesn't work that isn't anyone's fault. That's life.

It is marvellous that Stats SA should find that the country's manufacturing output grew by 3.9% year-on-year to January 31st when the growth for the December year was just 2%. The statistical office had a big job to do with a national census in 2011. University of Cape Town academics Tim Moultrie and Rob Dorrington suggest that the results of the R3.4bn survey contain so many apparent flaws and inconsistencies that their usefulness to government planners is highly questionable. Nevertheless, the Statistician General's (Pali Lehohla) contract has just been extended by three years with that office.

More GOOD news from the *Sunday Times* in volume terms in the middle of March. Manufacturing output grew 3.9% year-on-year in January whereas a month ago the figure for December was just 2%. Construction company Aveng reported headline earnings/share rose by 44% in the 6 months to end December. EOH Holdings reported a 39.3% rise, Howden Africa reported a 25.8% rise for the year, Amalgamated Appliance Holdings reports a 16% rise and Investec said that full-year earnings probably rose 17% after strong flows into its asset and wealth management arms. In the first increase since last September (post-Marikana), mining production grew 7.3% following an 8.9% year-on-year decrease in December. Offshore accounts picked up R2.1bn worth of Johannesburg Stock Exchange shares and R3bn worth of bonds. What wouldn't British Chancellor of the Exchequer George Osborne give for these figures in the U.K. economy?!

There is plenty more going right for South Africa in other sections of the economy. I was invited last spring to Summerhill Stud in the Land of Legends near Mooi River (www.summerhill.co.za). The establishment has been South African Champion breeder for the last eight consecutive seasons. Incorporated with the stud is Hartford House, voted *Best South African Restaurant, 2010, 2011,* and voted *Diners Club 'Diamond' Winelist, 2002-2011.* (www.hartford.co.za). I had never attended a Ready-to-Run preview before so was not quite sure what to expect. The venue was a miniature grandstand overlooking the stud's galloping track. The front terrace was laid out for owners, trainers and breeders to get a 'Pound-seat' view. Inside were tables laid out for a Hartford House lunch under Jackie Cameron, *chef d'équipe de la cuisine.*

Yearlings going for sale in the European environment are insufficiently mature to be asked to gallop in earnest and they are brought in from the paddocks in the summer before they get too frisky and incur any injury whilst at play with each other. In Ireland a century ago, Mr Edward Kennedy was visited at his Straffan Station Stud by that famous trainer Sam Darling. Mr Kennedy had a Fortunio colt out of a Pet mare that he had bought in England for 10 guineas. The owner's way of performing yearling 'trials' was to round up his produce one end of a very long field. He would suddenly crack his whip and off the bunch would go, occasionally hearing another crack o' the whip behind them. At the end of the gallop, the colt out of the Pet mare was leading. *"There you are, Sam,"* said Mr Kennedy, *"if you want to buy a certain winner for little money, go to the Dublin Sales and buy that fellow. You saw him beat the others. He always does."* Mr Darling thought 80gns. on the cheap side. The colt was sold on as a T-Y-O for £300 and won £14,000 worth of stakes for his next owner, Mr Gilpin. The story illustrates how things were done then, from just a tenner's worth.

It came as a surprise to me to see a statistical table illustrating the prices obtained at these Emperors Palace Ready-to-Run (RtR) sales.

In 2003 the average price obtained at the sales was R47,651. At the most recent event the average price was R228,187 – an annual increase of 37.9%. This also says that ten years ago it was necessary to take R50k to the sales which, @ R15 : £1 was £3,333. This time it was necessary, in round figures, to take £16,900 when the ZAR was R13.5 : £1. That's a 40.7% annual increase in the same decade.

The other 'benefiscal' (new word for OED!) feature of interest is South African Art. Bonhams held two auctions last year which grossed £7.5m with an average lot value of £45,000, previous world records being smashed in the process. With sales exceeding $18m in 2011, Bonhams is the global market leader in South African art. In pole position for their sale in March 2013 was the original portrait, 'Chinese Girl', by the late Vladimir Tretchikoff submitted by Ms Buhler's private Chicago gallery. Her mother, then the teenage daughter of a Chicago businessman, had acquired the painting for $2,000 from the artist whilst touring the USA in 1954. The large-scale lithographic print done by the artist became the highest selling art print in history, half a million large format reproductions being sold. The original picture which recently sold in London for £982,050 was expected to fetch £300-500,000. Bought by British diamond jewellery magnate Laurence Graff, the portrait of Monika Sing-Lee returns to South Africa after 62 years to be housed at the new owner's Delayer Graff Estate near Stellenbosch. The Chinese girl was working at her uncle's launderette at Seapoint, Cape Town when the artist begged her to let him paint her. She was paid £130 at 2013 prices for two weeks' modelling. The sale price equates approximately with 60 RtR racehorses!

Oh dear! There's some BAD news too. Employment remains a deep concern @ 25.6%. About 71% of South Africans between the ages of 15 and 34 are unemployed. Unemployment has risen by 100,000 between Q4-2012 and Q1-2013 when it was 24.9%. 3.5 million (33.5%) of people between the ages of 15 and 24 are unemployed and not in education or training during Q1, 2013. The number of discouraged work seekers has increased by 73,000 to 2.3 million. The Statistician-General said that unskilled and unemployed youth were unlikely to get jobs. "*They only time that they will get an income is when they reach 65, when they get state pensions.*" It is heartening to find that the biggest contributor to the increase in employment was the construction sector (+62,000 jobs). Finance and business services had an extra 37,000 jobs available and trade, 52,000. The agricultural sector shed 26,000 jobs, whilst opportunities in community/Social Services reduced by 22,000 jobs and jobs in manufacturing were 18,000 fewer. The Statistician-General spoke some home truths at the end of Q1.

1. The government has to put more effort into keeping children at school (too many drop out at Grade 10) and ensuring teachers do their work.
2. Unemployment could not be eliminated if the education system did not improve.
3. When the Matric pass mark is just 30%, employment is not going to follow.

A recent OECD report highlights that countries which have higher numbers of youth in their population have better prospects of growth than those with ageing populations. Just over a third of the SA population is under the age of 15. President Zuma said at the Commonwealth Conference on education and training of youth in Pretoria, "*We are certain that BRICS will contribute to satisfying the employment and development needs of our young population.*" I am not sure that many of the exasperated youth of South Africa would add a single brick to the wall that the President would like to build. Growth in retail sales slowed to 1.9%; dairy group *Clover* said that first-half earnings fell nearly 34% due to soaring production costs. As bulk milk goes by road, fuel hikes can only exacerbate the problem. The shares fell more than 2%. Underlying core earnings at *Gem Diamonds* fell 61% due to weak prices of 'a girl's best friend'. Agricultural supplier *Afgri* reported headline earnings for the last six months, down 15.2% due to significant poultry imports. Ready-to-roast frozen Christmas turkeys were imported from BRIC member, Brazil. The Johannesburg Stock Exchange reported a 15.4% drop in headline earnings from 555.9 to 470.2cts/share. Grant Thornton's *International Mining Report* showed that corruption and uncertainty over mining rights were two major concerns. Retailer *Verimark* advised that EPS for the year ended in February were likely to be down from 25.8c/share to somewhere in the range of 5.3 to 6.8c, a fall of at least 73.6%. Even shares in natural resource group *Coal of Africa* slid 16% after it reported an interim loss of $111.7m compared to $75m for the previous comparable period, a performance George

Osborne would wish to eschew.

The trade gap is often closed by FDI in good times. Times are hard now in early 2013. Some will find succour in Ernst & Young's new report on repositioning the South African investment case. 61% of 503 business leaders in 38 countries said that South Africa was in the top three African countries in which they would invest. 41% said SA was the most attractive country to invest in. Thus, SA is still the top FDI haven of the continent, but for how much longer? It is said that Nigeria, the country with the second highest reported number of cases of fraud in 2011, is catching up fast. The position of America as world leader is similar in many respects. The ramifications of lost confidence around the globe are widely felt, and questions are being asked about how much longer America can lead the world. American resilience, tenacity, initiative and pluck in the face of adversity is great.

Twenty percent of top business leaders said that Nigeria was in their top three and 6% placed it first. Exactly the same figures applied to Morocco whilst Egypt secured 3rd place (after two equals) and Kenya 4th. Put yourself in the plush leather seat in front of a spacious desk in a large office in London, Paris, Frankfurt, Strasbourg or New York as a 'fund manager' and you are looking for a home for €1-2m. Probably the longer you spend 'Googling' investment destinations, the more confused you will become. With so many traditional markets struggling, one must accept the evolutionary development of those Asian countries setting the pace. Emerging markets, as they are called because they have emerged into international reckoning since the 1980s and their pace of development bears out the old adage that success breeds success, India, China, Indonesia, Vietnam, Kenya, Turkey and Ghana – a mixed bunch geographically, bound together better than BRICS by positive structural factors. South Africa would have been mentioned but for the fact that the National Development Plan has been much touted, much discussed and is only advancing in hesitant stages when politicians concur with financiers. Trade, investment and infrastructure are factors which manifest themselves into Gross Domestic Product growth. Where there is growth, FDI follows. The latest hint is that government may not be able to fund the proposed infrastructure developments. P.S. China has just (08/07/13) decided to invest in Nigeria.

If the headline of the daily paper is not related to death and destruction by a runaway vehicle or a reckless driver killing several people at a time, the lead story is about some kind of violent (or non-violent) protest against conditions in the mining or agricultural sectors. The split between public and private sectors has grown massively over the first decade of the third millennium. Salaries for public servants have increased an average of 14% annually versus 2.7% in the period for all industry excluding agriculture. Minimum wage in the agricultural sector moved slightly ahead of Consumer Price Inflation (CPI) until the grievances of the seasonal workers in Western Cape came to light, followed by industrial action. Thence minimum wage jumped 54%, this figure being applied nationally, not just to seasonal workers. Inflation (5.9%) is at the upper end of the scale Trevor Manuel set of 3-6%. Shrewd observers concur with analysts that several other factors in the South African economy such as the trade deficit are not sustainable. Finance Minister Pravin Gordhan can only pay lip service to closing the gap between rich and poor. The government certainly has no intention of making the poor richer. It cannot even create the climate in which so many might have become employed due to the red tape surrounding business start-up.

The Statistician-General, Pali Lehohla, hogged the right and left columns of BUSINESS one day in May when he pronounced that the country would be better off with a youth wage subsidy than without. *"There is a problem of skills, a problem of experience and a problem of getting into the system."* The S-G put his finger on unskilled and unemployed youths being unlikely to get jobs when no extra jobs are being created by growth. He went on to identify 71% of the unemployed being between the ages of 15 and 34. Half that number, 3.5 million people, are between the ages of 15 and 24. Education is seen as the determining factor in gaining employment but if teachers are not there to teach, pupils are not on the learning ladder.

The latest statistics indicate that unemployment of those from 15 to 64 rose by 100,000 to 4.6 million between Q4, 2012 and Q1, 2013, or from 24.9 to 25.2 percent. During that same period the number of discouraged job seekers increased by 73,000 to 2.3 million. If one adds current work seekers to those who have stopped looking for work, the actual unemployment figure is well over one-third of the available workforce at 36.7%. It was not all bad news. Surprisingly the biggest contributor where there was an increase in employment was the agricultural sector which created 54,000 jobs. Government community and Social Services provided 44,000 extra jobs. Now it is time maybe to read this last paragraph again and weigh it against the APPOINTMENTS sector of *Business Day*.

Afrifocus want experienced equity Research Analysts. **Paton Personnel** want an IT Auditor, a regulatory reporting accountant in Investment Banking, a senior dealmaker in real estate project finance, corporate bankers, organisation design consultants, a quantity surveyor, and a corporate finance lawyer. **Next Leaders** require an experienced financial services recruitment consultant, a call centre sales manager, a digital specialist and some project managers. **D.A.V.** (professional placement) need a Sales Manager in liquid processing, an equity analyst, a retail manager for a franchise, a senior marketing and sales manager in JNB, a product support manager in the truck and bus sector. The **National Energy Regulator** requires a Financial Accountant who they will pay up to R531,143.72 per annum. **People Source** advertises 2 positions to join an existing team of Corporate Financiers, a CEO of Financial Services in Swaziland and a senior financial manager in investment banking. **The National Health Laboratory Service** seeks a Manager for a Histology service and a manager for clinical pathology. **TNS** seek a Field Manager – Market Research. At a glance one gains the impression that a country needing this scale of employees must be absolutely flying. Who do you believe?

Following the demise of the European market after 2008, little exploration East of Africa across the Indian Ocean has produced results. The President led a trade mission in that direction in 2011. All that the Indians and Chinese really want to know is how the infrastructure plans announced are developing across sub-Saharan Africa. It is one of their prime targets and if they get contracts they will be completed on time and within budget, using Chinese and Indian labour! The average remuneration of the CEOs of 326 listed companies and parastatals for that period was R4.76bn/year. Their average remuneration was R5.1bn in 2009.

It has worried me for some time that some readers with experience of all that is best in South African economics would perceive the author of being unduly sceptical and negative. After filing away SATRIX reports of the Exchange Traded Fund delivering 23.99% annual returns over three years and a staggering 36.8% over the past year, it is not the author but **Fin.24** that hoists the red flag, and so does Reserve Bank Governor, Gill Marcus.

Towards the end of July 2013 Eyal Sherel at Global Credit Ratings found that businesses that seemed to be healthy and flourishing a year ago are now starting to suffer or even collapse. The government has earmarked the Small Medium Enterprise (SME) sector as the key driver of growth, a matter that is replicated worldwide. Start small, make some money, recruit more labour, produce more goods, outgrow premises – EXPAND. Suffering and collapsing SMEs 'red flag' this sector of the economy insofar as job creation is concerned. Businesses took on more debt a year ago to continue funding aggressive growth strategy. With a slowing economy and the prospect of inflation and higher interest rates, deals have begun to fail. Personal experience is that it took one 'Blacksmith' (metal worker producing finished ironwork) three years to produce a quote for a pair of simple garden arches. When pressed on the matter a price was agreed and swift delivery one Friday afternoon was clearly implied. When seen in passing in the village the supplier claimed that he could not get 6m lengths of ½" round steel.

A second prospective supplier in the same *metier* produced a fractionally larger quote within two days and the arches within two weeks of anticipated delivery. It would appear that in rural areas these artisans have such full order books that orders for less than R1,000 take second place to the repair of farm machinery, engineering and general welding. An irrigation engineer advised that the best way to repair the leaking air pressure cylinder to our domestic water supply was to dispense with the old apparatus and install a new pressure pump under the house. The new pump did almost nothing and the R1,600 investment was reversed, cash paid when the supplier got paid by a dairyman who owes him money. This is Africa!

The slowing down of business in general is not confined to SMEs but across the industrial and commercial board. Taking on extra debt @ 14% has to be funded monthly come high water or low water. In 2012, 61% of employed people worked for a SME and those firms provide 52-57% of the country's GDP. Large, well-established listed companies have reserves to fund significant cash-flow and operational challenges, not so SMEs despite their eagerness to invest in the country. Global Credit Ratings experienced a record number of companies seeking funding for new projects in 2013. That there is an overall feeling in the operating environment that the future is not as rosy as the past, neither are employment prospects.

Gill Marcus warned at the Reserve Bank's AGM in Pretoria on Friday 26th July that the economy may not grow as fast as predicted. She cited electricity supply shortages as being most likely to act as a brake. The IMF has scaled South Africa's growth down to 2% from 2.8%. Growth in the other BRIC countries has also been scaled down. The Governor indicated that it was being overly simplistic to consider that emerging economies could assume a detachment from advanced economies. Last year's 2.5% growth was hampered by labour unrest, disruption of production, rising inflation expectations, falling commodity prices, electricity supply constraints and pessimism amongst foreign investors about the long-term outlook for the economy. The Reserve Bank set 3.3% as possible growth for 2014, depending upon what success Eskom meets with producing power even six months behind the previous schedule. The further delay at Medupi translates into a potential 700MW shortfall.

Despite the unrest in the mining and agricultural sectors in 2012, the number of working days lost decreased from 6.2 million in 2011 to 3.5 million in 2012. In the first quarter of 2013, 875,000 working days were lost, a 25% increase over the corresponding period of 2012. The Treasury wanted 7% growth to make a dent in unemployment. The President reduced that figure to 5% in his State of the Nation address. It will be interesting to learn what the governing party is going to say to the electorate next year.

Interesting days lie ahead for much has been planned against the general backdrop of worse-than-expected translation of forecasts into 'Actual' and credit downgrades by international assessors, Moodys, Fitch and Standard and Poors. Put simply, where 3.5% growth was expected, 2.5% had been delivered and someone is disappointed.

Mining-related products accounted for 25% of manufacturing output in 2012. Manufacturing is traditionally one of the country's biggest job creators. As a proportion of GDP, manufacturing halved from a peak of 24% in 1981 to 12%. Since liberation, manufacturing output averaged just 2.5% annual growth. To ameliorate performance, Gill Marcus called upon government to *"act coherently and exhibit strong and focused leadership from the top."* Brave woman! Is her job security dependent upon personal ability or, could she loose it at the whim of a politician resenting a call for leadership from the top when there is definite lack thereof?

Manufacturing is also suffering from the near-empty pockets in domestic households. This means that the bank gets first crack at a salary and only then can the worker see what is left in what is known as 'disposable income.' If the pay cheque is heavily garnished with debt, expenditure on manufactured goods is a 'no-go' area.

There are, of course, some bright lights shining. Production of iron ore is helped by increased demand from China, the world's largest consumer of ore. Why in God's name (and Allah be praised too) South Africa cannot convert more ore to steel and sell that to Asia, nobody knows. When in England large deposits of ore were found in the centre of the country at Corby, foundry workers were moved south from Scotland and 'British Steel' employed thousands. A slowing of economic growth in China might reduce that BRIC member's iron ore requirement. As far as steel manufacture is concerned, Corby died a long time ago. Many smaller firms have filled the vacuum attributable to the European Coal and Steel Consortium converting ore to steel more efficiently for less.

If one size fitted all there would be no mystery as to high interest rates are used in some countries and the lowest of interest rates are applied to the major economies. Some Scandinavian countries exercise the best fiscal management in Northern Europe whilst the South of Europe exposes the worst aspects of government mismanagement of the fiscus [from which comes the English term fiscal. It was the name of the personal treasury of the emperors of Rome]. A glance at the countries bordering the Mediterranean tells its own tale. Looking from east to west, Greece, Italy, Spain, Portugal lie between 35 and 45° North. Many of the most troubled Equatorial countries lie between the Equator and 10° North. Such matters are worthy of an academic Ph.D. Our grandchildren have just passed into university with sciences. It might appeal to them. The possibility exists that certain races possess better faculties for understanding finance than others. Was England really a 'nation of shopkeepers'? The profitability of leading supermarkets from time to time would certainly lead one to believe so. The smaller 'corner' shops appear to be in the hands of a multitude of darker-than-English skins who work hard to serve local needs.

To look at one South African province (out of 9) in seclusion might be skewed. KwaZulu-Natal, having such important places as Durban, Pietermaritzburg and Ladysmith reflects much that is 'South Africa'. The regional economy grew 23% year-on-year, after being in positive territory for the last three years. Struggling to overcome business problems can be stressful and a 'Stress' index reflects the negative factors such as inflation, employment and interest rates. The index grew 3.4% in the year and registered the largest increase since January 2013.

A local artisan of large character told a householder that his domestic water system would benefit from a booster pump to the gravity-fed supply. After requiring a R1,600 cash injection, he supplied a pump and left the householder to fit it himself. The pump failed to produce the expected result and the householder asked for a reimbursement in exchange for the return of the unit. The artisan promised payment as soon as a farmer paid him out of his monthly milk cheque. Women's Day public holiday delayed the matter another day and the exchange was laid on for the 6th day. The supplier arrived with a photocopy of a two-year-old invoice for the previous pump saying that his paperwork was devoid of when and how payments amounting to R1,000 had been made and wished to sort that out before exchanging cash for the unused pump. Printed paper proof for cash receipts paid into his account at the bank and other notes set the matter largely to rest pending verification with the supplier's accountant. The supplier paid over R750 of the money due.

The matter was supposed to be closed in two days. At the elapsed time, no telephone call, no payment until the supplier responded to an SMS suggesting that as he had to wait a long time in the past to be paid, the customer could wait too. If the allegation was true, fine! But it wasn't. Not only was the artisan wrong in implying, however courteously, that a previous bill might not have been fully paid, but he was wrong also in his failure to keep the appointment and pay what was owed if he could not find evidence to the contrary.

Now repeat this scenario a few hundred or thousand times between supplier and consumer across South Africa and the reason for retail sales being anticipated as 'flat' across the latter half of 2013 is more clearly understandable.

Contributing factors to 'Stress' were inflation reaching 5.5% in the province, a feature reflected countrywide and notified in a statement from the Treasury.

Inflation is the danger. It eats away at the consumer's purchasing power, it decreases consumer confidence and that affects business confidence in turn. This latter index was recorded at 83.6 points in 2005 and has fallen to '50' in the intervening eight years.

The second ingredient of the Stress Index is 'unemployment' which rose nationally to 25.6%, mid-2013. Locally it stood at 22% where 19.8 was reflected in 2012. A rise in the former is a rise in the latter. Stress, as a psychological factor, was brought home to me on a course in 1988 when participants were invited to identify recent events in their stressful lives. I scored highly. We had recently moved house, my mother died in Ireland amidst an unbelievable amount of acrimony and litigation. [She left her entire estate to a 'wicked' uncle and not a cent to anyone else.] Then my beloved 101-year-old Scottish-bred Australian grandmother died, having been a widow since 1925.

The antidote to stress was physical exercise and for how long it was taken. Cross-country running one day/week after the Pytchley Hunt and one day hunting the Albany Bassets was sufficient to counteract a house move, two deaths in the family, unemployment and a lot more. To those who are knotted up with stressful problems I say, *"Get on yer bike, boy" – "Get down to the gym, girl" – "Take that horse out for a couple of hours, lad" – "Get that vegetable patch dug over before you even dream of a pint in the local pub, man" – "Go belt a squash ball to shreds, lass"*.

Mike Schüssler of Economists.co.za produced histograms recording his Business Confidence Index, not only for Pietermaritzburg, the provincial capital, but for the province as a whole and the leading cities. The development of Durban has raised the index from 57.1 to 69.7 due to infrastructure upgrades (incl. Durban deep port and King Shaka airport). Confidence by the province as a whole has crept from 62.7 to 64.8 points. Port Shepstone shows a larger gain from 61.3 to 66.8. The one surprisingly bucking the trend is the port of Richards Bay. Business confidence there has taken a bigger knock than anywhere else, down 50% from 89.7 to 41.7. This is puzzling and the prime suspect is a 'short' year.

The sound barrier-breaking speed with which a number of aspects of South African life are moving has recently been confirmed by the President taking on the mantle of wizard of nuclear power. These

Zulus move fast. Remember, it is less than two centuries ago that they were still trading in beads and ivory tusks in many ports. Sir Christopher Wren (1632-1723) designer of London's St. Paul's Cathedral and many other churches after the Great Fire of London in 1666, also designed decimal currency. In this fire covering nearly 400 acres (180Ha) which started in a baker's house in Pudding Lane, behind Monument Yard, 88 churches were destroyed as well as the City Gates, the Royal Exchange, the Custom House, Guildhall, Sion College and many other public buildings. 13,200 houses were laid waste, 200 streets destroyed and 200,000 people were encamped in Islington and Highgate Fields to escape the four-day inferno in which only eight deaths were recorded.

The advance of South Africa into the nuclear age will not be as swift or traumatic as the Great Fire, the Blitz or the fire-bombing of German cities like Dresden during the latter part of WW2. It is, however, already having political repercussions just at the time when an inquiry into the last government purchasing fiasco is in great difficulty before it has even opened its wings.

The 2nd Arms Deal probe by the Seriti Commission was due to commence early August (2013). It had been announced in 2011 not long after the President's former financial advisor, Schabir Shaik, was convicted of corruption. This notoriety is brother of the one they nicknamed 'Chippy'. When he sought immigration to Australia, the interviewing officer is said to have given him the affirmative nod on the grounds that Australia needed carpenters! Presidential candidate Jacob Zuma had more items on his Charge Sheet than any other politician seeking any election in 2008 and he might well have earned the sobriquet 'Houdini', the American-Hungarian stunt performer famed for his sensational escape acts. These included being handcuffed, chained, roped and put in straightjacket under water. He escaped the lot. Fake magicians and spiritualists, however, did not escape his notice especially in America. President Zuma has escaped from more potential charges fringing upon criminal activity than any other national leader. For him to become leader of the African National Congress, a lot of charges were dropped and a lot of concessions made. The truth 'outs' eventually.

The first inquiry into massive bribery and corruption dated back to 1999. In the first week of the month in which we were all told to look out for Mars being its closest to Earth for 5,000 years, Judge Francis Legodi handed in his resignation. Two days later evidence leader Tayob Aboobaker, S.C., threatened to quit. He cited nepotism, unprofessionalism and infighting as suffocating reasons within the working environment.

This 2nd Commission was appointed by President Zuma in 2011 under Judge Willie Seriti and the researchers Mokgade Norman Maobi and Kate Painting because the scandal that reached the top of the political echelon simply would not go away. Ms Painting resigned, suggesting that the Chairman had a 'second agenda'. The 'hidden' agenda of the Commission might well have been to exonerate all South African politicians from any involvement in bribery to secure the totally unnecessary arms deal. President Zuma's legal adviser, Michael Hulley, and Justice Minister, Jeff Radebe, were despatched to talk to Judge Legodi but found that His Honour had already made up his mind. His departure for 'personal reasons', was promoted as backing for the integrity of the commission not being compromised. A very large number of people across several nations were involved in the deal. The Arms Deal started under Madiba's Presidency and quickly became a priority of his successor Thabo Mbeki who was succeeded by Jacob Zuma. Allegations of benefice permeate every level of government, the supreme 'Commander' of South Africa's armed forces not escaping. Loads of money passed hands to secure deals worth many billions of US$. The man who best captures my imagination is the bloke who so frightened the then new South African administration about national security that they believed they needed three worn-out German diesel-electric submarines and 26 Swedish Grippen fighter aircraft after the end of apartheid. A corvette or two, or three, made up the flotilla. One of the submarines broke down on the way down the Atlantic and had to be towed to its new base. Almost without break the submarines have been in dry dock in the former British naval station of Simon's Town. Twelve of the Grippen fighters are in mothball.

The term 'artful dodger' (Jack Dawkins in Charles Dickens's novel *Oliver Twist*) springs to mind when reviewing the careers of some of the top politicians in many countries. British Premier, Tony Blair, earned the sobriquet 'Teflon Tony'. Nothing stuck to him, except of course Ms Booth, Q.C., his wife, and 'loads o' money'. He was appointed the official Envoy of the Quartet on the Middle East. He has a 'soft spot' for Israel. The present conditions of Syria and Egypt are adequate testimony to his lack of success so why anyone pays to hear him speak is beyond me.

Just when the currency is doing the right thing for exporters, the very thing that neither KwaZulu Province nor the country can afford happened. The strike by the National Union of metalworkers of SA (NUMSA) affected 30,000 assembly line workers at Toyota's Durban plant alone. About 80% of Toyota employees nationwide joined the strike which meant at the beginning that the company was unable to deliver stock destined for 58 export clients spread over the rest of Africa and Europe. 16% of South Africa's manufacturing output comes from KwaZulu-Natal.

The strike came to an end at the beginning of October with the sort of *Mercury* Business Report headline that was easily anticipated: "*Full costs of motor strike will be felt for years.*" R500m in wages and benefits were lost by about 70,000 workers at some 150 automotive component manufacturing companies during the three weeks. Robert Houdet, executive director of that National Association, warned that the real impact would only be seen in two/three years' time when a factory closed down because a major export contract had not been renewed. Investors in South Africa prefer smooth running of processes in which they have invested shareholders' money. NUMSA claimed to have reached an agreement with the Retail Motor Industry Organisation to end the strike which crippled vehicle output because of the shortage of locally manufactured components. Having opened negotiations with a 20% increased wage demand in August and 8% and 7% for the ensuing two years, the union accepted a 10% pay rate with 8% in the next two years from major employers.

When new cars are planned, chosen component manufacturers are given seven- to eight-year contracts. Now that the labour environment in South Africa is becoming so unstable in industries varying from mining to vehicle production and viniculture, FDI is likely to go somewhere more stable. The damage has been done. Ford are having to airfreight components to Argentina and Thailand to prevent production stoppages because of component shortages. BMW – SA lost the opportunity to bid for the production of a new car model for the global market. They decided that the risk/reward for further investment during the current labour situation did not make sense. Irving Jim, General Secretary of NUMISA, feels strongly that BMW are blackmailing unions in an attempt to prevent further strikes in the industry.

Houdet's prophetic warning comes as the SA Revenue Services announced in the *Sunday Times* (Oct. 6) that the trade deficit widened unexpectedly to R19.05bn in August, the biggest gap in seven months. The latest figures come on the heels of a R14.21bn deficit in July. There is a massive shortfall in FDI following the revelation that offshore investors bought R912m of SA bonds and R131m of stocks in the week ended Sept. 27th. This R4.5bn of income for the month is just 23.6% of what is required. Could somebody please tell me how this 76.4% gap is going to be plugged?

Trade

In January of 2013, South Africa's trade deficit was five times (400%) greater than for the corresponding month of the previous year. The accumulation for the 12-month period was R132.54bn and countries normally rely on foreign direct investment in stocks and bonds to finance the gap. Financiers estimate that R703bn will be necessary over the next three years to do this @ R19.5bn/month. [R4.5bn/week]. In the immediate aftermath of the largest deficit on record, investors funded R4.2bn which almost, but not quite fills the gap. The deficit is expected to worsen, the rand is steadily weakening and investment opportunities are being snapped up despite some black natives not wanting foreigners to buy land or real estate.

If anyone can explain why South Africa needs to import R24.5bn worth of machinery, electrical appliances and mineral products which it cannot afford when exports for the month fell 11%, they should book an interview with the President or his Finance Minister. If either harboured the capacity to do anything they would stand on the Durban Port docks checking every weigh bill of goods arriving. If in any doubt that the appliance could just as easily be manufactured in South Africa, the container should be loaded back onto the ship and returned to the sender marked NOT WANTED – SUBSTANDARD. Nothing would please the 4.5 million unemployed more than to learn that they were to be given a job manufacturing to *Proudly South African* standards something that was being imported.

SA exported 47,075t of white maize to Mexico. It sounds a lot and it will be wonderful to receive the pesos, although difficult to see exactly what South Africa will do with them. In early June SARS (Revenue Services) showed that the trade deficit in April widened to R15.02bn, over double that of the previous month, because of increased imports. One sad aspect is that some of these imports will be purchased on credit by consumers who can no more afford them than the country can. In some cases they will be repossessed by the credit lender and sold for much less than they cost to import. *What to some is food, to others may be sharp poison.* Repossessions leave a very nasty taste.

The President did not report in his State of the Nation address his lowest trade deficit to please as many people as possible and that ANC is going to last until the return of Jesus Christ, a date which the President of ANC believes is infinite. Enlightened readers of *The Great Pyramid Decoded* [ISBN 1-85230-861-3] would put their money on 21st October 2039. The Finance Minister gave no motivation about exports in his Budget. South Africa is devoid of any leader with the country's best interests at heart except possibly Mr Motlante. One is 'feathering his nest' at Nkandla in the knowledge that trouble is brewing, the other has done so.

Political

The rumour that ANC finances are at a low ebb is fuelled by media reports that several employees in Lithuli House, their national HQ which is the former Royal Dutch Shell building, had not been paid their salary early in 2013. The party's finances are again under the microscope and may actually be in the red. If this is the case a massive fundraising effort will be needed if the party wants to mount an effective election campaign next year. In the autumn of 2013 the party was hell-bent on drawing attention to itself, cajoling the nation into believing that Madiba was well and in good spirits. The leader in *The Witness* written on Worker's Day (May 1st) spelt out the feeling of the people. LEAVE MADIBA IN PEACE. A publicity stunt and photo call was nothing more than vulgar electioneering. A frail ex-

President Mandela with a pillow propping up his head looked bewildered and undignified. Grinning politicians deluding themselves that they were there on a goodwill visit wanted only exposure of themselves at the expense of the man who gave their country 27 years of his life in prison for the cause of liberty.

KwaZulu-Natal Provincial Premier, Doctor Zweli Mkhize, who was elected party treasurer at Mangaung might be called to serve in Lithuli House in order to restore the party's finances to good order in preparation for the 2014 election. The ANC's constitution bars a person appointed to 'National' office from holding a 'Provincial' position of leadership. Mkhize would have to surrender his provincial post to avoid any conflict of interest whilst fundraising nationally. Two members of the executive committee, Willies Mchunu (Transport) and Nomusa Dube (Cooperative governance and traditional affairs), made veiled congratulatory remarks about the KZN Premier in recent speeches so, as W.H. Auden (1907-1973) wrote, *there's never smoke without fire*.

Second to Land Reform came the National Development Plan ushered in by ex-Finance Minister Trevor Manuel. The President said that 5% growth is needed to meet employment objectives. Funny thing there; a year ago government said that 7% was required to make a dent in unemployment. It makes one wonder. Who authorised the movement of the goal posts?

With education foremost in South Africa's hierarchy of needs, the President turned to teachers needing more remuneration and children more teaching. This is such old hat that blame can be laid squarely at the door of the governing party for failure to implement the necessary changes years ago. What happened when they first got into power? They fired the 'white' teachers.

Infrastructure development is trotted out every time a senior politician opens his/her mouth and you know what is said about the movement of the lips of politicians. Our little patch in the Southern Drakensberg foothills, 100 miles due west of Durban, is a microcosm of the nation in many respects. Two native generations ago a mule track followed the gorge of the Mkomazaza River taking supplies in and out of Lesotho. The arrival of the Land Rover and much road engineering led to a road being opened to Mkhotlong from Underberg. This path leads ultimately to Maseru on the west side of the old British protectorate of Bechuanaland. It is one of Prince Harry's favourite countries and his Sentebale Trust has done a massive amount to uplift the lives of the people who live as sparse an existence as Gurkha families in Nepal. The big difference – no pension from the Gurkha Welfare Trust. The continuity of British support for the old Protectorate is magnificent.

South Africa does not have the money to blow making a rough mountain track with 14 bends in the final 280m climb into a pristine tarmac road, safe in all weathers. R285m is reported publicly to have been spent on the first 14km over simple terrain through foothill farms. A 'leaked' figure suggests the figure was R400m more. Approval of a further R602m is awaited before the second phase can be commenced. The first phase was delivered three years late and four times over budget. Contractors are banking on the provincial (KZN) Department of Transport to approve the budget this year for the second phase taking tourists to the 2873m summit and Lesotho border post. Since the Department of Transport is barely capable of mending a pothole in any road, it will be surprising if it can muster the technical skills of the French, Swiss, Germans, Austrians and Italians to turn moving shale into fixed asphalt in the lifetime of any child in the district. That it will facilitate profitable export trade between Lesotho and Durban port is laughable. This is Africa!

Rumblings commence about workers being put out of jobs and they continue across the 'labour' spectrum for whatever the reason. In agriculture, it is the gradual laying off of 100,000 farm workers because of the rise in minimum wages. It is interesting to see a massive new Massey-Ferguson tractor parked on display outside a showroom that stocks Yamaha motor bikes and quad bikes. Greater mechanisation will take the place of unskilled labour in many instances at a time when the National Credit Regulator reports that the number of 18-34 year olds has grown significantly over the past year and more than 50% of all consumers are battling to pay their debts. Matching this bad news is the fact that the IMF has recently cut South Africa's economic growth forecast for 2014 by 19.5%, from 4.1% to 3.3%. Inflation is stubbornly at 5.9% and food prices are expected to grow by 9%.

Doctor Adrian Saville, Chief Investment Officer, Cannon Asset Managers, said in *Weekend Witness* at the end of February that his positive attitude towards economic growth for SA is based upon the fact that the country is so near and yet so far from being an investment haven of the quality of real Emerging Economies. Some sub-Saharan economies are amongst the fastest growing in the world. Where power supply, good infrastructure, well-organised logistics and a semblance of political stability prevails and there is no nationalisation in prospect, FDI follows. The technology sector of *Sunday Times* Business reported a couple of months later that even that small island in the Atlantic off the West Coast of Europe was open for South African Business.

Yes, the Celtic Tiger is back from the dead. Ireland got tarred with the same brush as Greece, Spain, Italy and Portugal but it never lost the significant image as a high-tech hub of innovation and employment. The Irish Development Authority facilitated the creation of nearly 13,000 new jobs last year and is well on the way to a repeat, or better, current performance in an economy of 4.5 million people. 14% of the 3.04 million labour force are unemployed, half that of Spain. The country is reckoned to have the 2nd most open economy in the world and exports 85% of what it produces. Software and service providers are in demand across the world. From Intel to IBM, and Google to Facebook, these major technology companies have core operations in Ireland. Business Connexion CTO Andy Brauer, Internet Solutions CTO Prenesh Padayachee, and *Sunday Times* 'Signpost' writer Arthur Goldstruck, arrived in Dublin prepared to deliver a lesson on Africa. Enterprise Ireland turned that around with the twin messages that Ireland is open for business, and that it has powerful lessons to offer any economy trying to shake off its high-tech slumber. The key to Irish success is close cooperation between government, universities and the business sector. Ireland is pro-entrepreneurship and pro-business and it has a supporting government that tries its utmost to create the right environment through both investment and education. Two-thirds of secondary school leavers go on to tertiary education. A country with scant mineral resources values all the more what it has – well-educated people. No wonder the designation 'Human Resources' became so important a decade or two ago. South African technological companies see themselves as offering a gateway to Europe. Ireland can provide South African countries with a better gateway to Europe. Enterprise Ireland's Fred Klinkenberg, who employs 13,000 people in South Africa, points out that Ireland and South Africa speak the same language, are close together in time zone and have a similar history in relation to colonialism. In the absence of SA being able to make its own impression on Europeans, it makes sense for South African business to team up with Irish technology and facilities to access European markets.

The investment manager's job and salary, to say nothing of the year-end bonus, is dependent upon accurate assessment of risk. The manager will know that South Africa's exports to sub-Saharan Africa grew 20.8% in 2012. Exports to the rest of the world grew just 1.6% (yr to March 2013) or on average of 1.7% over 2 years an abysmal performance.

But for poor education and struggling health care, South Africa could be living closer to its dream as the gateway from overseas to the internal markets of the continent. Big money has gone into Durban over the last 6-8 years and there is much evidence of freight movement. Alas, full containers are heading inland by the dozen and outward by the unit. Organised development by Transnet has to be of the same order as secure supply of power and reduced fear of nationalisation. The latest act in the latter field is the nationalisation of mining rights. The government would like closer control of banks and expropriation of farmland remains definitely on the cards. The ANC Party Conference at Mangaung ruled out mining itself and said that banks were off the list. Two steps forward, one step back.

The rand sank to R10.20 : $1 at the end of June. The President sought to reassure investors in the well-being of South Africa without actually saying anything positive to steady the money market. It is just coincidental that ZAR sank a further 2% that day and a further 1.5% the next day and that is no surprise for readers of the ANC-sponsored NEW AGE newspaper that ran a headline, *Economic growth shock*. Well it is a shock because there are so many small-to-middle-sized firms doing so well as regularly reported in the business sector of the financial press. This year's near-20% fall in the rand makes it the worst performing currency in the world behind Venezuela according to a Reuters report. The rand bounced back all right but that does not signal the end of uncertainty. One thing that markets don't like is volatility.

What economists have discovered is that GDP grew by 0.9% in the last quarter and by 1.9% year-on-year. The World Bank cut SA's growth outlook from 3.2% to 2.5% as concerns mount over continuing labour unrest in the mining sector in particular. The economic sectors failing to live up to expectations are electricity, water, manufacturing and agriculture. It is suggested that GDP for the year will have to be revised downward to below 2.4%. Whilst this figure would delight many Europeans (London included), it falls far below the 7% growth that the Treasury said last year would be necessary to make a dent in unemployment. The decline in growth cannot be any comfort to the 4.6 million who are looking for jobs and they fail to match the expectations raised by the President and supporting politicians when announcing such measures as the National Development Plan. The status quo remains for a lot of people on public support. Should the decline in the rand bring about inflation and the prices of staple foods increase, the public may start to look for answers. The fall in the rand comes as the annual wage bargaining season commences. Excessive wage demands may not be as excessive as first thought when the prices of basic foodstuffs are measured. Standing in a supermarket near the checkout is educational. There's money about all right, much of it belonging to the main banks and not to the person fishing it out of their hip pocket and peeling off a few R100 bills to give to the checkout operator. In the main the native worker is not particularly sophisticated as far as ingredients are concerned, so they buy first that which makes a tummy feel well fed.

We have been here before. The currency has crossed the R10 : US$ in the past, twice since we came to live here a decade ago. Nothing untoward happened and with the passing of time other markets weakened and confidence flowed back into the South African economy. There is something different about this time that has people thinking that the recovery is unlikely to become visible for some time. Put together as ingredients of a cocktail, high unemployment, rising inflation, job dissatisfaction, unhappy miners, farmers shedding labour, too narrow a tax base for welfare benefit and the country's power supplier falling behind with ability to produce enough electricity, and you have a mixture that certainly should not be stirred or shaken, certainly not as James Bond desired. On 30th May Eskom had a reserve margin of 1.6% compared with international best practice of 10-15%. Well, isn't it lucky that recent growth has been 0.9% and not 5 to 7% as needed!

Fin24, South Africa's premier site for up-to-date business and finance news, stock market data, economic analysis, personal finance and investment information has surveyed ordinary South Africans' debt. Precisely 624 out of 32,000 respondents (2.06%) have no debt. Most alarming is the fact that almost 425 respondents spend 80% of their income on repaying debt. One twelfth of those surveyed spend their entire income on debt and 7.8% have debt repayments which exceed their income. Debt is being incurred on a monthly basis to pay for food, transport, electricity and water. Well this is certainly another matter that The President omitted from his State of the Nation address.

It is interesting to find that Fin24 categorises earners of R10,000 to R30,000/month as middle and high-income earners who, according to debt expert Moeshfieka Botha *"simply cannot manage their finances"*. The level at which South Africans are incurring debt has reached fever pitch and much of it is unsecured. Annabel Bishop, an Investec economist, finds that the average household has 31.8% more debt than a year ago. An increasing number of people are applying for debt counselling and Roger Brown, of a firm in that field called *Credit Matters*, warns that unless consumers become proactive about their debt, they will end up losing the assets that they have purchased on credit. People are taking too long to seek help and time is against them. For many the 'bomb' will explode sooner than expected.

The Chartered Institute for Purchasing and Supply Africa and the Bureau for Economic Research at Stellenbosch University run a monthly survey called the Kagiso Purchasing Managers Index. [The UK equivalent, the Manufacturers' Purchasing Index, is currently at a 14-month high.] The PMI measures business confidence. On a scale of 0-100, below 50 indicates contraction and above it shows expansion. For the last two months (April-May, 2013) the figure has been 50.4 – not an 'expansion' signal. The new sales orders index stands at 51.1 (previously 53.7) and the Business Activity Index stands at 50.6 (52.2). The Employment Index ended the month of May at 47.2 (42.1), still significantly below the key 50-point mark. The report ends on the chilling note that recent moderation of the Producer Price Index could be reversed in the coming months due to inflationary factors. The picture is not as pretty as a rural landscape on a frosty morning.

CHAPTER XV

EDUCATION

The World Economic Forum revealed in its Global Information Technology report, 2013, that only one country out of the 144 studied had a worse record than South Africa in the assessment of the quality of maths and science. Singapore leads the world, Zimbabwe holds 50th position, Swaziland 110th, Mozambique 131st and the next country to host the FIFA World Cup is the only country below South Africa (Yemen). South Africa's education quality was ranked 140/144. It would be wonderful to think that the special task team recently established by the Minister of Basic Education to investigate the progress of teaching programmes in maths, science and technology would produce results within the year. Not only is the country bereft of the ability to create employment, but those who seek employment lack basic skills. Four million uneducated, unemployed youths on the streets of South Africa is a very dangerous situation. A mid-April 2013 *Witness* headline read **School violence surge**. Back in 2008 the Centre for Justice and Crime Prevention found that 22% of secondary school pupils had succumbed to some form of violence in the preceding 12 months. The latest report shows that 22.2% of high school pupils had been threatened with violence or been victims of assault, robbery and/or sexual assault during the previous year. The number of pupils assaulted increased from 3.7% in 2008 to 8.2% most recently. Violence in schools was most prevalent in the Free State and Western Cape with Eastern Cape and Gauteng being the safest areas. Declining moral standards in society, TV and misunderstandings in the home where parental support is lacking were singled out by the report as prime causes of the surge in school violence.

There is enormous worldwide variation in the attitude of governments to education. I well remember when The Hon. Penelope Verney-Cave was a student of Warwick University telling me of her studies into the matter and that many perceived education of the vanquished or colonised as a dangerous thing, as learning enabled people to think. Those who after WW2 thought it expedient to copy former imperial colonialists and subjugate an indigenous population through an apartheid system were only in it for themselves. They lacked some elements of human intelligence. Intelligence comes primarily from education, genes, experience, good habitat and food quality. Humans are born with slightly varying amounts of brain material which absorbs all of the above. The better the wholescale environment that the child is raised in, the greater the ability of the brain to absorb, store and apply the data. A stark difference in government priority exists between two of the nations 'liberated' from peer oppression seven decades apart in C.20th. Since the Irish Troubles (struggle) successive Irish governments have poured national wealth into schools and universities with the result that the modern Irish workforce is the recipient of much Foreign Direct Investment (FDI) that might have gone elsewhere in Europe. Within two generations Ireland became the hub of 'intelligent' industries like computing and pharmaceuticals.

Every so often there is a glimmer of hope from a report that four maths whizz-kids, two from Maritzburg College and two from Cape Town, are engaged in the Bulgarian International Mathematics competition at the end of June. None are higher than Grade 10, the time when so many drop out of education with just two grades to go for matriculation.

The President has stated that the time that teachers must spend in classrooms must rise from 60%. This may be every bit as important as that spent listening to their Matric-eager pupils. Close on the heels of this idea is realisation that scholastic achievement is going to lead to employment where a government can point to opportunities arising from both growth and FDI. Current growth is less than 3% and Treasury advises that 7% is necessary to make a dent in unemployment. It is extremely difficult to see where jobs are going to come from to a better educated workforce if the government spends an excessive amount on unnecessary imports and the trade gap is left in deficit by lack of FDI. Why, for example, must the country import

46,000t of beef whilst so much state grassland goes to waste?

Government is presently closing down rural schools many of which were started by local farmers. Despite education being the country's greatest need and beneficiary of the largest chunk of the national budget, no provision has been made for these children's future education.

Our 17-year-old grandson in Ireland has expressed a keen desire to be an engineer. He has been accepted by Liverpool University aged 21 to read sociology after declining the possibility of a Commission in the Irish Guards. I have yet to learn of a better training ground for general engineering than growing up on a farm. There is always something to design an improvement on, be it the rainwater run-off from an avenue, the placing of a drinking trough for cattle, the hanging of a gate or clearing the tractor's fuel system from fuel contamination. Military service personnel go through courses of instruction in many functions. A course with the Royal Engineers at Gillingham, Kent, stood me is sufficient good stead half a century later to understand that SAPS had failed to kettle the crowd on the koppie at Marikana on 16th August 2012. They did the job in broad daylight with antiquated equipment immediately in front of the miners instead of preparing the job by night and ensuring proper encirclement. It is possible that there would not be a Commission of Inquiry into the deaths of 34 miners at one time if the job had been done properly.

Nuts and bolts of change was a *Witness* (May 27) article of interest in engineering that caught my eye. The picture showed a couple of native engineering students preparing to drill metal. Only 14% of professional engineers registered with the national Engineering Council are natives. A great improvement has already taken place in 20 years for there was then no formal registration. 47% of those seeking to become professional engineers are native. The author abhors the generalisation of people by colour, black or white. The situation is not so clear cut and is a grey area. Indigenous natives are chocolate (it doesn't matter if it is milk or plain). The descendants of settlers, new arrivals and Swallows are generally 'white' with varying shades of pink and fawn, a few *rooineks* occurring amongst the latter off the Durban beaches after too long exposure to the elements.

Those studying engineering technology form 72% of candidates and the proportion of native students aspiring to engineering degrees and diplomas has risen to 60%. Germany (*vorsprung dur technik*) leads the world in terms of numbers of engineers with 200 per capita of population. Brazil (where many *Volkswagen* are produced) comes second with 227, and in the U.K. (*former home of Rolls Royce, British Leyland, et al*) there are 310 engineers p.c. for 3rd place.

Here in South Africa where there is only one engineer per 3,100 people the situation is improving most in the province of KwaZulu-Natal. Lesedi Consulting Engineers [Est. 2010] has been creating employment and offering mentorship to help engineering students to complete their studies; 40% of the employees are women and 70% are 'youth'. The small engineering companies are drawing students from higher educational establishments. In the decade since 2000 the number of engineering graduates has increased from 3,100 to almost 10,000, or 22.25%/year.

Politics

The non-event of the 2nd month of the 14th year of the 3rd millennium was the pomp and pageantry leading to the abysmal performance by President Zuma in trying to tell Parliament what the State of the Nation is. The red-carpet treatment was afforded all attending this Cape Town event. Mounted police on some pretty flighty-looking equines followed expensive motor bike riders, blue flashing lights ablaze. In the wake of a 21-gun salute, the largest number fired for the highest of State occasions, the people of South Africa could have expected to hear something fresh from their President. He failed them.

The President advised his parliamentarians that he harboured a bout of 'flu and asked to be excused any sniffling and below-par delivery of his address. He was probably a far better stick fighter and herd-boy than student of English. His rise to fame is no match for past world leaders like Margaret Thatcher, the daughter of a Grantham grocer who became the first lady Prime Minister of England for over 11 years. Nothing could excuse the mediocrity of the faltering English that was expressed. In the last five years no ophthalmic consultant has managed to fit the President's spectacles to the distance between the bridge of his nose and the apex of his ear lobe. This necessitates the poor man continually having to adjust his reading glassed so that they do not feel as though they are going to drop forwards. The significant matters trotted out could more accurately be described as 'own goals' than new scores. Most had been heard before.

President Zuma would prefer to dwell most upon the downside of the colonial and apartheid era, drawing upon issues that can be made excuses for non-delivery 19 years after the commencement of democracy in 1994. There were far more natives than settlers so why only 482 Voortrekkers were killed in the Bloukrans massacre on 17th February, 1838, is anyone's guess. Less than 60 years later the Zulus showed their military ability when annihilating the 24th Regiment at Isandlwana. Why did they not do it again whilst the British force was so weakened? They could have rid the country of the colonial oppression so many resent to this day. It is all very well President Zuma blaming the past for his problems. Like *Bafana Bafana*, the national football team, he frequently has the ball at his feet but cannot see the goal. Given a golf driver, he misses the ball with his first swing and puts it in the rough with his second. Much laughter and merry making, but no political clout when it matters.

Corruption received the usual airing during the President's address. The sustained poaching of rhinos (277, or 2.7/day) this year to mid-April, particularly in the country's premier National Park, probably gets a nod and a wink from a Minister pretty close to the President. The American apolitical organisation, *Avaaz*, was shocked to find the figure as high as 1.6/day a year ago. Talking to the Vietnamese and others of South-Eastern Asia is probably as useful as talking to the trees in Kruger National Park. One is reminded of the lyrics from *'Paint your Wagon'*, sung by Bones McNally, Lee Marvin and Clint Eastwood in various editions, *"I talk to the trees but they don't listen to me…"* The only sign of anyone listening in Asia would be a fall-off of rhino poaching. A culture so deeply ingrained is not going to be repaired as quick as a puncture.

Health got a mention though no figures as to what people will pay into a National Health Scheme emerged and thus there was no indication as to exactly what the money would fund. There are probably a number of health centres as well run as the clinic at Underberg. Their excellence is attributable to a few dedicated senior nursing staff. The tentacles of 'Transformation' are ever present and the most experienced of radiologists is to be replaced by one who will have to send X-rays to another hospital for interpretation and vital information for doctors and patients may not be available for days, especially at weekends. As ever, there is a bad apple in the barrel. A nurse advised that she would be on the Christmas holiday period rota told her senior that she would 'go sick'!

Back in the chamber of parliament, it was apparent that many delegates were bored by the repetitive trotting out of the same platitudes and promises that they had heard before, yet they applauded as they relished hearing them again. One of the few giggles the President got – and he giggles a lot himself – was when, under the heading of health, he referred to obesity. Some whose Body Mass Index far exceeded the norm sat very still and stony-faced. For the health of the country, obesity was probably the most important part of the State of the Nation address.

Did the President tell the people that the country is going broke, importing far more than it exports, and that Foreign Direct Investment is not plugging the gap? 'Corse 'e didn't, 'e ain't daft!

CHAPTER XVI

SUMMARY

The reader is now well versed in both the history of the main indigenous protagonists from the earliest identifiable historical beginnings (rather than myth and legend) to modern times. Readers of European or Asian history may ask what was going on in South Africa during the Han Dynasty that coincided with Roman Britain, or the Ming Dynasty which covered English medieval Kings from Richard II to the Restoration of the Monarchy under Charles II following Oliver Cromwell's (The Protector) flirtation with Republicanism. He was the first and last ruler to execute an English Monarch.

It was during the Ming Dynasty (1368-1662) that the Portuguese took a liking to the coast of East Africa (particularly Delagoa Bay), the Dutch to spices from Indonesia and English sailors claimed land as theirs wherever they could put into port unopposed. The author has put into the book much learned in South Africa since first visiting Johannesburg in 1995. When visiting the Southern Drakensberg region six years later at Christmas time it seemed that it was time to take advantage of the opportunity to buy land for cattle at a quarter of the cost of European 'turf'. The rand was sliding from R15 : £1 and touched R18 near the time a farm was transferred. We paid about £65 / acre for 932 acres. Some may be offended that so little is mentioned of the broad cross-section of white settler families and developers of land, or of the Boers and Afrikaners. Few of these three categories make up much of modern South African history or play an important political role now. When countries become liberated the nationalist spirit emerges to the fore and they place their own people in the positions of the former oppressor even to the point of the national language being required for government employment. This was easier for Mr De Valera to impose in Ireland than would be in a country of 11 official languages, English being predominant for commerce and law, French being the language of the diplomatic corps.

Some call it transformation, some indigenisation. The former might be applied to someone wanting all Springboks to be indigenous natives; the latter would cover the transformation of foreign-owned business in Zimbabwe to national ownership. The net result is that whenever possible the native supplants the foreigner regardless of the extent to which the latter feels part of the nation and being a South African; well, just as native of the country as the natives except for skin colour. Very few whites achieve the distinction of being honoured as a white Zulu as was the case with the late David Rattray.

A new nation such as one that has known liberation and democracy for less than two decades still needs external help even if only to pay for some of the raw materials which have to be imported because they do not exist locally. Advances in agriculture necessitate the importation of foreign-made machinery, and so, we go back to the drawing board – of trade. If South Africa had been Japan the country would have bought one of each agricultural implement and replicated it as many times as the market demanded. Where beads and metal arm bands bought elephant tusks 180 years ago, fresh fruit pays for Italian *Landini* tractors and *Pedrollo* water pumps.

More advanced societies have funds from profits generated in their own countries which they invest in developing nations to reap further profits and create wealth. For a European, Asian or American to profit from investment in Africa it is necessary to find a company already involved in one of the continent's emerging economies. This is Foreign Direct Investment (FDI). It can vary from investment in shares on the local stock exchange to money being transferred monthly from the Pensions Service to pensioners who have emigrated from Britain and taken up residence overseas. The British government did the dirty on a large number of people who after contributing all their working lives in Britain, later decided to retire abroad, many to Commonwealth countries. The Government 'froze' for good the amount payable at the rate at which it was first paid out. This meant that there is no built-in inflationary factor and thus if

£107.80 was the first payment, that is the amount that will be paid weekly until death. At no point in any employee's career and monthly deductions by the employer for National Insurance contributions did any employee ever receive any notice to the effect that if they retired abroad, their State Pension might be jeopardised by not being linked to inflation. The £107.80 might have been worth £150 by 2014.

Suppose an average exchange rate of R12 : £1. The pension when first paid would have yielded R1,293.60 in South Africa. Ten years on it is still that amount yet at 6% local inflation the same pensioner needs R2,455.64. Freezing the pensions of UK and Irish citizens who worked in Britain and retired to Commonwealth countries must rank amongst the most scurrilous, dishonest actions of Tony Blair's administration. British pensioners inject a wealth of FDI into South Africa, yet it is not enough. South Africa is sliding down the scale of investment destinations and only received $4.57bn in 2012, a drop from the previous year. In that time, South Africa dropped four places in the FDI Confidence Index, from 11th to 15th of 28 countries. As for comparison with its BRICS peers, China is 2nd behind USA. Brazil is 3rd, India 5th and Russia 11th.

The African continent has enjoyed FDI growth since 2010, attracting the third most investment after Nigeria and Mozambique. The investments in the latter countries were largely in oil, gas and mining. The range of investments were more diverse being in pharmaceuticals, mining, finance, manufacturing and tourism, much of it in new businesses. President Obama and his team discussed Afro-American trade, believing that it would help in dealing with the effects of slow economic growth and high unemployment in both countries. R130bn of trade was done between the two in 2011 with more than 600 US companies being involved and over 12,000 people being employed. Edgars Stores have belonged to Bain Capital since 2007. Paulson & Co own $1.2bn worth of Anglo-Gold Ashanti and much of Massmart belongs to US giant retailer WalMart. Revolution of one kind or another, peaceful or violent, is going to influence the minds of foreign investors in Africa as a whole.

Many journalists, the indigenous, pragmatic ones in particular, frequently let slip in an article something about the quality of the country's leadership. It was noted at the time of the De Doorns disturbances in the Western Cape wine-growing district that the

Minister for Labour was out of the country. At the time of Marikana the President was out of the country attending a South African Development Community summit and when the Gupta family's aircraft landed illegally at Waterkloof SADF airbase for a family wedding at Sun City, "No. 1" was out of the country. The ANC recalled the academic Thabo Mbeki at Polokwane because they thought that his interests lay elsewhere and that Jacob Zuma would do a better job. Now he and his ministers are enjoying the perks of foreign travel.

The perception of investment in South Africa has been marred by bad news from the country. The bravest of investors are probably the American hunters who come here to shoot wildlife, much of it penned in on game farms and not totally wild. Globalisation of the media implies that anything of significance on SABC News may be picked up by SKY and FOX News. David Rattray's murder shook the world and reminded it that *"This is Africa"*. The repercussions of the massacre at Marikana by South African police on 16th August 2012 triggered SKY correspondent Alex Crawford to enquire if the country had learned anything in the past four decades. Well that police element certainly had not and you would have to meet the rural police to appreciate how totally different they are. Constable Ncgobo's few sheep are our rough grass mowers.

Two British Airways and one South African Airways jumbo jets plus others fly between South Africa, the Middle East and Europe every day. Most of the 300 passengers on board will have stories to tell when they get home. It will possibly have seemed strange to many that every evening South Africans are told to switch off their swimming pool pumps and immersion heaters (Geysers) for a few hours to conserve the nation's power. People don't use their pools in mid-winter and switching a Geyser ON and OFF consumes more electricity than leaving the apparatus on a thermostat set at 50°C. Humans like to bath and shower in 43°C, no mix with cold water being necessary [Eskom do not accept these facts!]. In early July, the coldest part of winter is yet to come, a situation similar to the British Isles (Geog.) and those parts of Western Europe most affected by the Gulf Stream in early February. The warming of the Gulf of Mexico manifests into the emergence of snowdrops and narcissi closely followed by the first spring blossoms. Nature has a wonderful way of taking one's mind off the fact that the national supplier may have a supply crisis at any moment. Would you invest in a country likely to run out of power when alternative better prospects existed in France or Japan?

Cecily Camona, principal at A T Kearney (global management consultants) watches South African growth closely. Dritus Combrinck, portfolio manager at P S G Konsult is also reported in the *Sunday Times* (June 30) as pinpointing education and training as holding the country back from expanding out of the presently restrictive infrastructure capacity. Constraints are envisaged with roads, water and sanitation and lack of adequate labour skills. Pressing for higher wages impinges upon the country's attractiveness as an investor target. There are also a number of bright spots in the renewable energy sector and Stanlib manages a private equity fund exploring the market with R500m of start-up capital. There is greater investor confidence in these above-ground fields than there is down the mines now that the current selling price of the principal precious metals is below the cost of production.

The Arab Spring has thrown up a number of surprises, the most recent of which is that democratically elected President Mohammed Morsi was toppled a year later. The people created such mayhem in Tahrir Square that the Army had to intervene and put the Moslem Brotherhood leader under house arrest. If the Egyptians are the only ones unhappy about Islamic political expansion, why are so many mosques being 'bombed' from the Middle East to England? I've just realised! We all know the answer. Religion has caused more loss of life than any other human trait.

An early-July report from the South African Press Association in Johannesburg told readers of *The Witness* that President Zuma's approval levels in urban areas have stabilised close to their lowest point since the last general election. In the middle two weeks of May 2013, TNS (Global Market Research) found the President's rating to be 42%, one point better than a quarter earlier. The percentage rating is the portion of 2,000 adults in the country's seven major metropolitan areas who believe that the president is doing a good job. The ANC shocked a lot of people when their leaders tried to make political capital out of a visit and photo call on ailing and weak former President Mandela. The cameras did not support the line that the old Madiba was sitting up and well. It was deeply distressing for his family and for many South Africans. Claiming on radio that Madiba had said that the ANC is doing well did not go down well with those who have read in the media that he is on a life-support machine at Medi Clinic heart hospital, Pretoria.

The many found 'sitting on the fence' by TNS could step off in either direction. Up to 31% were undecided about the President in 2009. Two years later this fell to 14% and has wavered recently. A 42% approval rate is a weak starting point at the run-up to a general election. Deputy President Kgalema Motlanthe was charged by the President with leading talks between unions and mining houses. Should the Deputy President be successful in finding long-term solutions for the industry and stand for Presidency in 2014 the red carpet could be rolled out for him. He is of totally different political manner and stature to Jacob Zuma. He commands a lot of respect for his political ability and quiet approach to any given situation. Where some might have panicked at AMCU refusing to sign the framework agreement for a sustainable mining industry on 3rd July, the DP calmly recognised that the contents of the document were not in dispute and that the Association had a requirement to go back and consult its members.

With ailing ex-President Mandela surviving on a life-support machine, the end beckons and the nation prays for his peaceful transit to the world in which he will surely be recognised as the greatest of the ancestors. There are no doubt medical histories of the will to live prevailing longer and the patient giving the family a brief reprieve from the inevitable. An enormous upsurge of grief will be widely expressed. He served South Africa as Sir Winston Churchill did England. He 'touched' a lot of people's lives during his term running the South African revolution. It is tragic that so much of his life was spent on Robben Island. The country must move on, no analysis, debrief or 'post mortem' being necessary. It will be great for the country if his legacy should translate into the country regaining lost momentum for the people are worthy of great success in their rapid transformation from the pastoral warrior of 200 years ago into the advanced well-educated society of the wider world. South Africa epitomises **'the beauty and the beast'**. Raw beauty of landscape and wildlife, excellent roads and magnificent coastline. This book is also a tribute to my friends and acquaintances Rob Guy, David Rattray, Dan Knight and Ian Fellows who met violent deaths at the hands of natives.

SOUTH AFRICA: REFLECTIONS ON A REVOLUTION

I am very grateful to the South African government for granting us Permanent Residency Permits to live there for 13 years. I shared the love and friendship of many good friends both native and of settled stock. I had no greater friend than my late wife Wendy (neé Spencer), who so bravely suffered the injury caused by a running dog shattering her right leg, fracturing her left hip, having a mild stroke, major back surgery and much subsequent illness. She died at Himeville in 2013. Her ashes were scattered by our eldest son Piers, in Winwick Churchyard, Northamptonshire, where we were married in 1964, and he was christened in 1965.

A few days after the liberation of Paris from four years of German occupation, Edith Piaf, whose talent was already evident, performed at the Moulin Rouge night club with Yves Montand, a newcomer chosen to appear with her.

As said of the show, *Moulin Rouge,* and equally applicable to South Africa…

"Another hero, another mindless crime,

Behind the curtain, in the pantomime,

On and on, does anybody know what we are living for?

Whatever happens, We leave it all to chance;

Another heartache, another failed romance,

On and on, does anybody know what we are living for?

The show must go on,

The show <u>must</u> go on.

Outside the dawn is breaking

On the stage

That holds our final destiny

The show must go on,

The show <u>must</u> go on.

Inside my heart is breaking

My make-up may be flaking
But my smile still stays on.

In memory of Madiba
The show <u>must</u> go on.

I'll top the bill, I'll earn the kill,
I have to find the will to
carry on with the show
The show **must** go on!"

Credit: Brian May, of 'Queen'.

EPILOGUE

South Africa went on after the last curtain fell at the Moulin Rouge, the Parisian show that has titivated millions over the years. Life only stops when the doctor, paramedic or veterinary surgeon can obtain no further responses to any of the senses, such as pulse or the contraction of the iris.

Such is not the case with vibrant, if politically and economically shaky, South Africa three years after this book about its revolution was started. The country became a lot more violent, in contrast to the pair of Egyptian geese and their six goslings grazing peacefully on the dam wall 100m from where I write. The tranquillity of rural southern Drakensberg is rudely interrupted by a scarlet monoplane spraying the adjacent crop of maize. Three hairy Jack Russell terriers are trying to make out the whereabouts of a predator that roamed the garden last night. It is surely the same genet that has recently wiped out my entire population of chickens and bantams. No longer is the prospect of dawn heralded by *Tweedle Dee* who was hatched two years ago in a TIPPOO China tureen strategically placed in the *Belling* hot cupboard.

Mduduzi Mzolo, my handyman/gardener (note, not 'boy') brought to the kitchen door one morning a clutch of eight freshly hatched bantam chicks in a nest, on top of which lay their dead mother, possibly the casualty of a puff adder. We hatched off the two remaining eggs and named them *Tweedle dum* and *Tweedle dee*.

The same man has just done a great job with the assistance of my maid in cleaning congealed sulphur from the chimney of the AGA cooker. Few know that the famous letters stand for Acetylene Gas Accumulator. The stove stores heat and its perpetual warmth permeates a house, especially if the kitchen door is left open and the main bedroom is above the kitchen. The cooker was designed and invented in the 1920s by Gustav Dalen (1869-1937), a Nobel Prize-winning physicist. He also designed the flashing mechanism used in lighthouses and navigation buoys. He won the contract to illuminate the Panama Canal. With Gustav de Laval he invented (1892) the milk fat tester that some are so obsessed with today for healthy food.

Much of Dalen's early work was done in his Swedish Villa Ekbacken due to him having lost his sight in a gas pressure explosion in 1912, the year his brother Albin received the Nobel Prize for physics on his behalf. Dalen was also instrumental in the invention of the Iron Lung.

Enough of European domestic inventions, study reveals that invention is not part of the national psyche, a matter that provokes thought. Mduduzi Mzolo has watched me at work in the garden, at plumbing and carpentry for a decade. I can now leave every job on the small holding in his capable hands. The Zulu child appears artistic and the wire toys they make give them great satisfaction. They are the only toys they have in most cases.

Government leadership in this and so many fields is lacking. For 10 years I have submitted to journals the thought that this or that could be manufactured in South Africa. A voice in the wilderness if ever one was heard.

The world has lost confidence in the rainbow nation. Investors worldwide look to other emerging countries for better returns. The five-month platinum miner's strike was the first to set things back and when Amplats reported a 46% plunge in annual profits, investors caught on. Amplats went on to sell off non-performing assets as they struggled to recover from the strike. Returning to pre-strike output levels will take time and CEO Mark Cutefani aims for a return on capital of at least 15%. A 20% drop in the platinum price over six months due to weak demand from Europe thwarted some objectives. The shares dropped below R320 in the run-up to Christmas. Accounting for 38% of the world's platinum output, the conglomerate soon showed that it was one of the majors that would rebound swiftly and it did so.

Much of this was written on my kitchen steps on the south-east side of the house. Firstly, it is cooler there and secondly, I wanted to write directly into 'Word'. No such luck, no power. Necessity being the mother of invention, I like running water but it would only run when there is electrical power to the *Pedrollo* pump that sucks water from the donga from the dam and pumps it 100m to the house. I installed on a 2m platform a 1,500lt *JoJo* tank with a 2.8m head which is sufficient for a gentle flow into the house by gravity in the absence of electrical power. It is only necessary to turn a Chinese-made Venice ball-valve tap one way until the electricity comes back on. Why does South Africa have to have taps made overseas when they could manufacture them at home?

South Africa became a member of BRICS (Brazil, Russia, India, China and SA) to enhance trade and share technological innovation. Of these countries only India was recording appropriate commercial success. For its part South Africa was only achieving a trade surplus once in three of the last 24 months. The record deficit in January 2015 beat the previous record (October 2014) by 15.6%. Much of the country's trade deficit was attributable to R5bn worth of machinery, R2bn worth of vehicle components, R1.5bn of base metals and R1.2bn of chemicals. I can think of no good reason why VENICE or Tivoli should have taps made in China or Italy respectively when they could well be made in South Africa. Likewise, the importation of so much machinery and vehicle components in an economy of so many job-seekers. The South African native is perfectly capable of doing a lot more than government has ever asked of him/her. Leadership and education are sorely absent. The country is leaderless and 'Education' is as backward as it was in the apartheid era, if not more so. A national leader would import skills before machinery and double investment in education. If 30% of the goods imported when the currency is so weak could be manufactured in the country, it is possible that unemployment would fall by 3 million. Just think how that would stimulate the domestic economy!

The word on everyone's lips at the beginning of 2015 is one that has been there for too long. To call the management of Eskom at Megawatt Park, Johannesburg, a bunch of cowboys would be grossly insulting to that fine breed of Americans and Australians who ride beautifully, treat their horses carefully and are good stockmen. It would also be a little unfair to CEO Tshediso Matona although the man is 'short' on power and even shorter on recognising who pays his salary. The important decisions about the national power utility are taken in Luthuli House, HQ of the ANC.

The word 'ineptocracy' crept into the Oxford Dictionary of

descriptions of South African politicians in 2014. Ineptocracy prevails throughout Parliament with very few exceptions. It is also true that young nations give jobs first to the political faithful, particularly if they were associated with the 'Struggle'. Only two Eskom executives (Maroka and Dames) in the last decade had ever spent a day of their working lives in either power generation or power distribution. The rest of the Board members who take mammoth emoluments are political stooges who have no place in national corporate governance.

To keep everyone sweet the government agreed to give Eskom a R20m bail-out to help finance its R225bn shortfall. The national energy regulator is supposed to ensure that Eskom conducts its business and the best interests of its customers for the long-term sustainability of the industry. On the front of an Eskom info pack issued in 2008, the slogan says: "Easy to do business with". Many municipalities have found Eskom so easy to do business with that they have run up debts of R50bn. Eskom gives no reason for not collecting the debts and no reason for not policing properly thousands of illegal connections where people steal electricity from the grid. In its despair to gather funds, Eskom will disconnect a 75-year-old widower who has a contract to pay regularly in order to get him to pay faster. A contract is a contract anywhere except with Eskom. The ability of personnel to read mail, or of subcontractors to read meters properly, is highly questionable.

At the heart of any economy is the economic generation of the national power supply. Generating stations are close to the resources used to create the heat to run the turbines. The power stations of South Africa are on top of the coal fields and they have plenty of the black stuff for years to come. Power stations and nuclear reactors take a long time to bring to power production. The government may have learned a lesson from not planning ahead adequately, the situation affecting the country for the first half of 2015. There was talk then of South Africa having already signed a deal with Russia for the provision of nuclear energy to create electricity. Politicians like to learn of their place at the trough and the construction of nuclear power provides food for thought. Some may ask 'how can we cream from this one as much as we did over the Arms deal?' Remember 24 useless Grippen fighter aircraft and three diesel-electric submarines. Why useless? Because, like a tub of yoghurt that tastes fizzy, they were beyond their sell-by date. Oh, I nearly forgot. The aircraft became too expensive to fly and the submarines have hardly ever left Simon's Town naval base, the home to many British Royal Navy personnel in a bygone era. This is Africaaaaaa!

There's another crisis in South Africa

The country learned to hold its head up under Nelson Mandela. It became stable under Thabo Mbeki when we went to live there. He was recalled by the African National Congress at Polokwane and the man who said that HIV-Aids could be washed off in a shower after sex was made President. Jacob Zuma prevaricates and is economical with the truth in his State of the Nation addresses. The ANC do not have a better icon than the laughing, smiling, joking, dancing, charismatic Zulu leader.

Don't mistake me. The man has four wives and a lot going for him. He is the front man of a political group whose power is ebbing by the day. The Democratic Alliance and the Economic Freedom Fighters have the usual electioneering fight on their hands. What do parties losing their grip do? They cling on for dear life! Causing instability and uncertainty in the ranks of those who feed the country inures thoughts of Dublin-born author and English Statesman Edmund Burke (1729-1797) who wrote in *Thoughts and Details in Scarcity*, "And having looked to Government for bread, on the very first scarcity they will turn and bite the hand that fed them." His best known literary work is *'Reflections on a Revolution in France'*. He died aged 68 in the middle of the most bloody part, the year after King Louis XVII died in prison and Kildare-born Catholic emancipation supporter, Wolfe Tone, tried to land at Christmas-time with French troops in Bantry Bay.

White South Africans are people from South Africa who are of European descent and who do not regard themselves, or are not regarded as, being part of another racial group (for example, as Coloured). In linguistic, cultural and historical terms, they are generally divided into the Afrikaans-speaking descendants of the Dutch East India Company's original settlers, known as Afrikaners, and the Anglophone descendants of predominantly British colonists. In 2011, 61% were native Afrikaans speakers, 36% were native English speakers, and 3% spoke another language as their mother tongue such as Portuguese or German. White South Africans are by far the largest European-descended population group in Africa. White South Africans differ significantly from other white African groups, because they have developed nationhood, as in the case of the Afrikaners, who established a distinct language, culture and faith in Africa. In the 2014 National Census, they were 8.4% of the population. Today, white South Africans are also considered to be the last major white population group of European ancestry on the African continent, due in part to the mass exodus of colonials from most other African states during regional decolonization like that of Kenya, Rhodesia and Uganda. Whites continue to play a role in the South African economy and across the political spectrum. Eton College has always been a source of political leaders, viz; Harold Macmillan, David Cameron, Boris Johnson and Church-leader Justin Welby, Archbishop of Canterbury. Add to this illustrious list old Etonian Toby Chance, currently Democratic Alliance M.P. for Soweto West, Shadow Minister for Small Business, and you might be excused for saying, "*Well there's hope for South Africa yet!*"

Now, 20th March 2017, White South Africans, especially the Afrikaners, face perhaps the greatest threat to their existence in centuries on the continent after South African President Jacob Zuma recently came out in support of confiscating white-owned property without compensation.

There are well-founded fears of "genocide" against white South Africans amid reports of surging crime, especially against farmers. White South Africans face even more race-based laws and regulations than existed under apartheid, driving minority white South Africans out of the economy and forcing many into squalid squatter camps.

Christian missionary Charl van Wyk saw the hate directed against the Christian Afrikaners with his own eyes in 1993 when terrorists burst into St. James Church and killed 11 people. Van Wyk opened fire with his own sidearm, startling the terrorists who expected nothing but unarmed victims, and causing them to flee. He recounted his experiences in "Shooting Back: The Right and Duty of Self-Defence." Now, he is calling for a spiritual awakening among his people, the Afrikaners.

"It was not language or country of origin which primarily dominated Afrikaner identity – for there were Dutch, German and French speakers," van Wyk said of the Afrikaners. Nor was it his geographical position, as they were living across the Cape, Orange Free State, the Transvaal Republic and the Republic of Natalia. The name comes from the Nativity. The prominent landmark of the Bluff was sighted by Portuguese explorer, Vasco da Gama when he sailed past it but did not land on Christmas Day 1497.

The Christian faith is what distinguished the Boer. The further the Afrikaner has moved away from his love and relationship with his God of the Bible and focused on land, language and skin colour, the more his Christian identity has been eroded. The most important historical attribute of the Boer (Afrikaner) was the fact that he was Christian! Visit the Parish of Drakensberg community of St. Michael's and you will travel a long way to find anywhere more Christian and less Boer. It is a dairy, beef and corn area. If it follows the pattern of most of the rest of land redistribution, the province of Natal containing the major cities of Durban and Pietermaritzburg, will go hungry. Durban got its name from Cape Colony Governor of 1835, Sir Benjamin d'Urban. His was an old Huguenot name. Boer leaders Piet Retief and Gerrit Maritz each gave part of their names to Pietermaritzburg. Robert Mugabe (Zimbabwe President) and Jacob Zuma drink from the same cup. It has been said that South Africa is not safe in the hands of Jacob Zuma.

His response: President Jacob Zuma of South Africa has ruled out a Zimbabwe-style takeover of swathes of the white-owned economy and dismissed a push for nationalisation of the crucial mining industry to resolve the country's gaping inequalities. What JZ did not say anything about is how he came to support **confiscation of white-owned property without compensation.**

"Nationalisation is not the ANC policy," said the President to Damien McElroy in a London *Daily Telegraph* interview in his official Pretoria residence in December 2012. That was four months after Marikana and considerable industrial unrest in the run-up to the 2014 Election in which the newly-formed Economic Freedom Fighters party under former ANC Youth Leader Julius Malema, took 25 of the 400 National Assembly seats and 6.35% of votes in their very first election.

It is now March 2017 and the President has overcome a lot of dissent with his leadership. A man has needs. A woman has needs. A country has needs. I submit that the last thing that South Africa needs is uncertainty, instability and the appearance to the outside world that national problems can be resolved Zimbabwe – style. Oh yes. The show will go on – African-style.

*

I undertook to bring the reader up to date with Current events. In a telephone conversation with an eminent settled South African cattle and sheep breeder and ex-international polo player who has sufficient confidence in his enterprise to buy neighbouring land, no matter came across more clearly than 'Corruption'. Just as cream settles at the top of a milk bottle, so corruption has settled at the top of government, where personal enrichment from public resources is now called "State Capture".

The Democratic Alliance has discovered that the Public Protector, Busisiwe Mkhwebane, recently held discussions with The President's legal advisers on the ABSA Bank / Bankorp bail out. Annexures to the supplementary affidavit of the SA Reserve Bank demonstrate that the Public Protector does not act impartially but takes orders from Union Buildings, Pretoria. The DA calls for her removal from office under section 194 of the Constitution dealing with misconduct, incapacity or incompetence. Her track record is not in her favour.

In his speech in Utrecht, (the Netherlands one!), Avicenna Leadership Award winner Mmusi Maimane said *"Nothing has undermined our new democracy more than the evil scourge of corruption which had been underpinned by the grand project of capturing the State for the purpose of personal enrichment"* - *"we cannot secure a better future until we crush the evil corruption in our present. It is time to liberate ourselves from the liberators. We must seek to break the cycle of corruption and maladministration before there is nothing left on which to rebuild South Africa."*

In the 2nd half of last year (2016) the Gauteng High Court found that the decision to discontinue the prosecution of President Zuma in order to enable the ANC to call him to high office was irrational and illegal. The Court set the original decision aside thus effectively re-instating the 783 charges against him. President Zuma and the National Prosecuting Authority were refused leave to appeal by the High Court. So, they petitioned the Supreme Court of Appeal and got a hearing.

They appeared before Judge Mahomed Navsa on 14th September ultimo. The DA's report on the hearing gives every indication that the original decision to prosecute Jacob Zuma still stands. The Judge was of the opinion that the original prosecution was not a bad one and he concluded *"all that remains is that the decision to prosecute is reinstated."* President Zuma may yet get his day in court. It will take weeks, or even months for the Supreme Court of Appeal to deliver its formal verdict. Even after that the Defendant could appeal to the Constitutional Court, but with no guarantee of success. You have read so far. We go to print. Stay tuned to www.dailymaverick.co.za/article/Zumaincourt, or Google "South African Supreme Court of Appeal on Jacob Zuma".

Who better to conclude this analysis of the beautiful but tempestuous South Africa than ex- Nationalist Apartheid era Premier, F.W. de Klerk? He was interviewed on Radio Eireann last week and the highlights of what he had to say were:

- Almost everything in South Africa is now being orientated on race.
- Light at the end of the tunnel due to President Zuma stepping down in December.
- The need for the country to return to the Mandela Legacy of racial harmony and tolerance.
- In the 8th vote of 'No Confidence' in The President's leadership, 25-30 ANC M.Ps. voted 'Yes'.
- Change in leadership is 1st step to realign an investor friendly climate.
- New leaders must focus on fiscal recovery.
- ANC divided into 3 sects. 1. Communist, 2. Black Nationalist, 3. Old moderates - old values.
- Economic Freedom Fighters (EFF and Julius Malema) seek greater progress for blacks.
- If ANC falls below 50% of vote, EFF will form a coalition with them to gain power.
- ANC will remain the biggest party with a much reduced share of the vote.

- Some whites do not believe there is a future, the rest accept a rough period ahead.
- Whites are emigrating and thus becoming a shrinking minority.
- The National Prosecuting Authority could be compromised to prevent charges against The President which were dropped to facilitate him becoming leader, being reinstated.
- There is a dearth of World leaders with the ability to think beyond their term.
- Donald Trump criticised for lacking in depth and for his approach to serious problems.

THE END

SEQUEL

In mid-summer 2017 an overnight thunderstorm reminds one of the climate in which one lived for 13½ years, 100 miles due west of Durban. A look at the South African news reminds one that *"plus ça change, plus c'est la meme chose."* South Africa swings from one extreme to the other. A photo by Philip Magakoe, one of the photographers at Marikana, portrays a President in distress though denying any impropriety or wrongdoing. No change there either!

The 75-year-old President faces continuous pressure to step down. He is unlikely to do so whilst President Mugabe holds office. Zuma raised the ire of landowners and farmers recently by suggesting confiscations without compensation. I just wonder where he got that idea?! It would please a small number of natives who want land but don't actually want the stress of farming it commercially. Tending a few cattle and goats while the women fetch water and firewood, as they tend the children, is much more the lifestyle of the indigenous African male.

As the corruption profile of the country rises to the detriment of the people in general, the President faces renewed pressure to step down. In June 2017 over 100,000 documents and e-mails were leaked to reporters. They appeared to detail improper dealings with the Gupta family. This family of Indian origin have lived in South Africa for decades and have become VERY influential. It was for them that an Indian civilian airliner was allowed special permission from "someone high up" to land at Waterkloof SAAF military airbase in 2014, bringing Gupta family and friends to a wedding at nearby Sun City. Thus, they all bypassed 'immigration' at O.R Tambo International airport, Johannesburg. At the subsequent inquiry nobody was able to name the "someone high up" but it cannot have been far from a desk near the President's office. He attended the wedding.

The African National Congress (ANC) led the fight against apartheid and came to power under former convict, Nelson Mandela. 'Madiba', as he was affectionately known by his clan name, saw the birth of the 'rainbow nation' and handed the baby in the bath to Thabo Mbeki in June 1999. In 2008 the ANC recalled him at the Polokwane Conference in favour of Jacob Zuma. Thus commenced the demise of modern South Africa.

Splits in political factions occur all over the world except possibly in Eastern Asia, North Korea and China. The present split in the ANC is largely due to personal greed. The President allocated well over R200m (US$16m+) of the public purse to his private means at his Nkandla homestead and got away with it. A brutal and avaricious bid for wealth and power, in lieu of sticking to idealism and ethics for the benefit of the people leaves one thinking *"Zimbabwe, here we come!"*

The first question answered is, *"Who's to follow?"* The name of Deputy President Cyril Ramaphosa comes first to most lips. His only real blemish as a successful businessman is that he protested about the striking miners the day before Marikana and sent e-mails to two Ministers and to Lonmin advocating "concomitant action." Mud did not stick because he was considered right to have called for action. He would not, however, have had mass murder by the police in his mind.

Professor Anthony Butler, University of Cape Town, describes the ANC as being *"in very big trouble."* Shrewd and successful 'Black Diamond' as he is, Cyril Ramaphosa practises better ethics without being tarred with the brush of corruption. A lot of this is 'par for the course' of politics. Look at the trouble Mrs May is in following the Brexit vote landing her a nasty job and a vote of confidence not being carried by the electorate.

Last autumn (March 2017) tens of thousands of people protested against Zuma for sacking the greatly trusted Pravin Gordhan. The credit rating agencies, Standard and Poors, Moodys and Fitch reduced the South African economy to 'Junk' status as a result of this breach of confidence in a most trustworthy Minister. His fault: not agreeing with the President!

One finds in our summer/their SA winter, that the economy is officially in recession, unemployment @ 27.7% of the 20 million possible employees has hit a 14-year high. There is no prospect of economic growth improving and all the 'plans' announced are waylaid by the ANC's focus upon internal politics. The race to the top in December 2017 appears to be between Ramaphosa and the President's first wife Nkosazana Dlamini-Zuma. Maybe that country also needs a woman at the helm. This 68-year-old lady was an anti-apartheid activist, Minister for Health 1994-1999, and then Minister for Foreign Affairs under Thabo Mbeki and Deputy President Kgalema Motlanthe. Her ex-husband moved her to Home Affairs in his first term. In 2012 Dlamini-Zuma became Chairperson of the African Union Commission, which post she held for almost 5 years. Since 2015, she is largely understood to be favoured by her 'Ex' to succeed him as President of the ANC and as President of South Africa. Mr Zuma would thus remain in control of the ANC and the State, thus avoiding prosecution for still-pending criminal charges. Wily old fox! The new party leader will face Parliamentary elections due in 2019. This book sets the scene for some very exciting times and much drama in store in this wonderful land. He has just survived, by 21/384 votes with 9 abstentions, the 8th vote of no confidence in his leadership. The ANC will probably recall him from party leadership in December 2017 and his term as National President must end in December 2019. A new party leader will face Parliamentary elections due in 2019. You thought South Africa interesting. Try South African politics! This book records the history and sets the scene for some very exciting times and much drama in store in this wonderful land.

©McGILLYCUDDY@NENAGH ON 19.07.17.

D-DAY: A new platoon of Front in front of the miners gathered a grazing sweep UNDERSTAND, KEVIN STUFFER

SOUTH AFRICA: REFLECTIONS ON A REVOLUTION

Relatives of the miners killed at Marikana on August 16 watch a video of the day of the shooting at the Farlam Inquiry in Rustenburg yesterday. PHOTOS: FELIX DLANGAMANDLA

SOUTH AFRICA: REFLECTIONS ON A REVOLUTION

Striking mineworkers protest in Marikana on September 5, 2012. The Anglo American Platinum mining company, the world's largest platinum producer, announced yesterday that it will close four mine shafts and sell one mine, expecting to cut some 14 000 jobs.

PHOTO: AP

Rebecca Milcao said loan sharks and buying on credit from local spaza shops had been part of his existence since coming to the Rustenburg platinum belt 14 years ago.

"Without them, life could virtually come to a standstill," he said. "It is hard to repay the loan, but what can you do? We know that even our supervisors need to take these loans."

Milcao, a labourer at Lonmin's Saffy shaft, said he was worried about his mother in a village outside Maputo, Mozambique, because he had not been able to save enough to visit her since the strike last year.

"I bought her a cellphone so that we could communicate," he said. "Although the network could be troublesome, at least I would know they are well and they will also know that I am well here."

But he had not heard from her for a while.

"I don't know what has happened to the cellphone because I can't reach her any more. I think they are so broke. Broke!" he said.

Milcao said he was managing to save some money and he hoped to have enough by December so that he could spend Christmas with his mother and his two children in his village.

"I have had a lot of people to pay since we returned to work. It has been tough, but I am making headway and I am planning to finish [repaying] my loans and groceries debt by this month end — even if it means being left without a penny in my pocket," he said.

But for Lethabo Matlaku, one of the youngest men on the workforce and a new recruit, life is good. He had been unemployed for a long time in his home town of Sebokeng in the Vaal Triangle, but now he has a job operating a *makaranyana* — a small train carrying ore in the shafts — at the Karee mine.

"It is always good to have money," he said, even though working underground was "not a very good job".

"I am still adjusting to the conditions, particularly breathing," he said. "I was already here when the violence started. It was horrible, but I couldn't do anything because I needed the job and the money. Some of my homies in Sebokeng don't believe that I am working in the mine — underground, for that matter," he said.

The future of mining remains unsettled. The word underground, according to some miners, was that rock-drill operators at the Karee mine were planning another strike. It could happen as early as this week.

VELD MEMORIAL: Crosses dot the koppie near the Nkaneng informal settlement in Marikana to remember the 34 miners who lost their lives. Picture: DANIEL BORN

Protesting miners dash for cover as a policeman shoots at them at Marikana two years ago. PICTURE: REUTERS

Ramaphosa on the back foot

CYRIL Ramaphosa must still be smarting from the taunts and heckles from protesters branding him a scheming and callous politician-cum-businessman who orchestrated the Marikana massacre.

This happened while the lawyers of the widows and relatives of the slain Marikana miners went for the jugular, calling for Ramaphosa to be charged in the International Criminal Court.

Chants of, "You killed them for profit," "You are a sell-out," "Capitalists are using you," and "Buffalo head," repeatedly rang at the Farlam Commission of Inquiry while Ramaphosa was testifying.

He also finally got the opportunity to clarify the context of his e-mails imploring two former ministers to act against the striking mineworkers.

"I did want to come and tell an account of what my involvement is. I am rather pleased that I have managed to tell the people of our country how I acted in all this," Ramaphosa told journalists on Tuesday.

But he might view his decision to send the e-mails as a fatal error of judgement. For a man widely esteemed as an urbane and shrewd politician, his indiscretion is an episode he may wish to erase.

For starters, this is the leader who took the tactical decision to stay away from active politics for almost two decades after machinations within the ANC top leadership thwarted his presidential ambitions in favour of Thabo Mbeki. So any association with the Marikana massacre is not the type of indignity he would have liked in his political comeback.

Never mind his other imprudence when he unsuccessfully bid for an R18 million buffalo.

He said the heckling "was no big deal".

"When you are a leader, you must expect that there will be people who do not like you. People will throw rotten eggs at you, that's par for the course."

Political analysts Somadoda Fikeni and Aubrey Matshiqi agree that Ramaphosa has suffered bad public perceptions, but they don't think Marikana will have a serious impact on his political career.

"Yes, it might have been an exercise to influence. But generally, commissions in South Africa don't have as much impact as we assign them. It's unlikely that this will have any impact on him."

He said Ramaphosa's experience with a constitutional democracy and the fact he emerged from the ANC's traditions would ensure he triumphed over adversity.

"Some may compare the current leaders within the ANC and say we prefer a person with a background as a unionist and constitutional development."

There were negative perceptions about the buffalo bid.

"The major perception Ramaphosa has to deal with was the blunder of a buffalo."

He said the bid reinforced the perception about leaders neglecting the people while they lived large.

"That is why (the lawyer for the injured Marikana miners) Dali Mpofu couldn't resist the temptation of going for the jugular."

Matshiqi concurred, saying Ramaphosa now had to deal with the negative perceptions about him as a capitalist.

"It reinforces the perception that he was invited to be a (Lonmin) board member simply because they can benefit from political influence. Hence, the accusation that he is a sell-out," Matshiqi said.

"People like Dali went there to win a political battle, as a leader of the EFF. The amount of time Mpofu spent on Ramaphosa's e-mails was an attempt to portray the deputy president in a negative political way, as a leader of ANC not more than an errant boy. In my own assessment, Ramaphosa suffered at the level of perception and in the court of public opinion."

He said while there might be some within the SACP and Cosatu who might view Ramaphosa "as a lackey of white capital" this would do him little harm.

"The question is whether that will prejudice him in his presidential ambitions. It's too early to tell. But who becomes the president of the ANC is not dependent on the commission." There have been calls for a woman to succeed Zuma. Both Matshiqi and Fikeni said even this would do little to thwart Ramaphosa's ambitions.

"I am not sure about the idea of electing a woman as president yet... If the female candidate is (AU commission chairwoman) Nkosazana Dlamini Zuma, does the ANC want another Zuma? There may be opposition from those who think that the ANC might be entering the sphere of dynastic politics," said Matshiqi.

LEGAL RESOURCES CENTRE

NPO No. 023-004   PBO No. 930003292

Constitutional Litigation Unit • 16th Floor Bram Fischer Towers • 20 Albert Street • Marshalltown, Johannesburg 2001 • South Africa • www.lrc.org.za
PO Box 9495 • Johannesburg 2000 • South Africa • Tel: (011) 836 9831 • Fax: (011) 834 4273

Your Ref:
Our Ref: G Bizos/Nkele

26 November 2012

Mr Donough McGillycuddy
PO Box 95
Himeville
KwaZulu-Natal
3256
Email: mcgillycuddy1@isat.co.za

Dear Mr McGillycuddy,

Thank you for your assessment. You have obviously followed the proceedings. Your articulate analysis will be of great value to us in our cross-examination of the senior police officers. We will use the questions and arguments you advance. They will find it difficult to answer them. We will lead evidence of experts in crowd control.

Please continue your interest in what is happening at the Commission hearings. Don't stop letting us know your views.

Sincerely

George Bizos
George Bizos

Sunday Times | June 28 2015
Seconds before the shots that changed South Africa

A policeman takes aim at protesting miners near Lonmin's Marikana platinum mine, Rustenburg, on August 16 2012. When the shooting eventually stopped, 34 miners lay dead or dying. In the days before the massacre, an estimated 3 000 miners had gathered on a rocky outcrop near the mine in a wildcat strike. PICTURE: REUTERS

SOUTH AFRICA: REFLECTIONS ON A REVOLUTION

ON THE EVE OF DEATH: Mgcineni Noki, in his green blanket, shortly before he was killed at Marikana

BRUTE FORCE: Police approach dead and wounded miners after the shootings. Military assault weapons have no place in law enforcement, a security expert testified at the Marikana commission hearings
PICTURE: KEVIN SUTHERLAND

Housekeeper, Saraphina Radebe, in traditional Zulu dress in front of the Author's house.

The author and the late Madam McGillycuddy.

Hodgson's Peaks, Southern Drakensberg, from the author's home.

Ian and Gill Dyer venture into the Indian Ocean.

The author, Donough McGillycuddy.

Sorrel, the author's English bred hairy JR awaits her bath.

Saraphina Radebe, our Housekeeper (Domestic).

Dr Gaynor Cartwright, Chiropractor, 'Forever Friend', and her daughter Stephanie.

Printed in Poland
by Amazon Fulfillment
Poland Sp. z o.o., Wrocław